PIXAR
THE OFFICIAL
COOKBOOK

PIXAR

THE OFFICIAL COOKBOOK

TEXT BY **S. T. BENDE**

RECIPES BY **TARA THEOHARIS**

INSIGHT
EDITIONS

SAN RAFAEL · LOS ANGELES · LONDON

CONTENTS

CHAPTER THREE:
ADVANCES IN TECHNOLOGY

2010–2019

CHAPTER FOUR:
THE LEGACY CONTINUES

2020-TODAY

INTRODUCTION

———————— ★ ————————

As one of the most innovative creative animation studios of our time, Pixar has become an integral part of our shared cultural experience. Their films are emotional powerhouses, with frames filled with heartwarming heroes and timelessly touching themes. But it's Pixar's commitment to continued creative advancement that truly sets it apart from its contemporaries.

The studio's origins date back to 1979, when computer scientist Ed Catmull joined the Lucasfilm Computer Division. Working alongside John Lasseter, Catmull focused on building the digital filmmaking tools that ultimately grew into what we now know as computer graphics. When Steve Jobs purchased Lucasfilm's computer graphics division in 1986, the newly created Pixar would eventually develop the technology it would need to create the world's very first computer-animated film. Each subsequent movie has proven more innovative than the last, as Pixar storytellers continue to push themselves to new heights. With creative story techniques and ever-emerging technology, Pixar truly embraces the wisdom of its iconic character, *The Incredibles*' Edna Mode: "Never look back, darling. It distracts from the now."

From the moment it burst into our hearts with its very first short film, *The Adventures of André & Wally B.*, Pixar has captivated moviegoers everywhere. Whether learning how to fall with style alongside a Space Ranger and a cowboy, or cheering for an arrogant race car and his plucky, tow truck best friend, Pixar has taught us all to embrace adventure, to find joy in the unexpected, and to believe in the all-encompassing power of friendship. In *Pixar: The Official Cookbook* we'll explore the ways that food ties those themes together . . . then dive deeper into some of the films that are especially rich in culinary culture. Through spotlights on *Ratatouille*, *Turning Red*, *Cars*, *Toy Story*, *Coco*, and *Luca*, we'll examine the way that Pixar has utilized food to push their stories forward, while simultaneously pulling characters together—over a good meal, of course! From finding acceptance at a new friend's dinner table (*Luca*) to the happy memories evoked by a beloved childhood meal (*Ratatouille*), Pixar knows how to portray all aspects of the human experience while tugging on our heartstrings in the best possible way. Buzz once urged us to reach "to infinity and beyond!" Pixar has unequivocally done just that . . . and our world is all the better for it.

Throughout its storied history, Pixar has utilized food as a tool by which its characters experience key moments. From Remy's emotional response to combining strawberries and cheese in *Ratatouille* to Jin's thoughtful presentation of his lovingly crafted stir fry in *Turning Red*, food is the thread that weaves many of Pixar's most heartwarming moments together. And through this cultivated culinary collection, we can now bring the feeling of those universal Pixar moments into our very own homes. With eighty-four all-new dishes inspired by Pixar's iconic films and shorts, *Pixar: The Official Cookbook* brings families together in a whole new way. And with recipes ranging from Nothing Fishy Vegetarian Sushi Rolls (page 55) (*Finding Nemo*) to Scream Factory Hot Wings (page 47) (*Monsters, Inc.*), this book truly has something for everyone. Whether the littlest sous chefs among us embrace these new dishes with a cheerful, "Mine, mine, mine!" or push their plates away with a firm, "Put that thing back where it came from or so help me," the memories that are sure to come from cooking together and sharing meals around the family table are truly timeless. Just like Pixar itself.

TIMELINE OF PIXAR FILMS & SHORTS

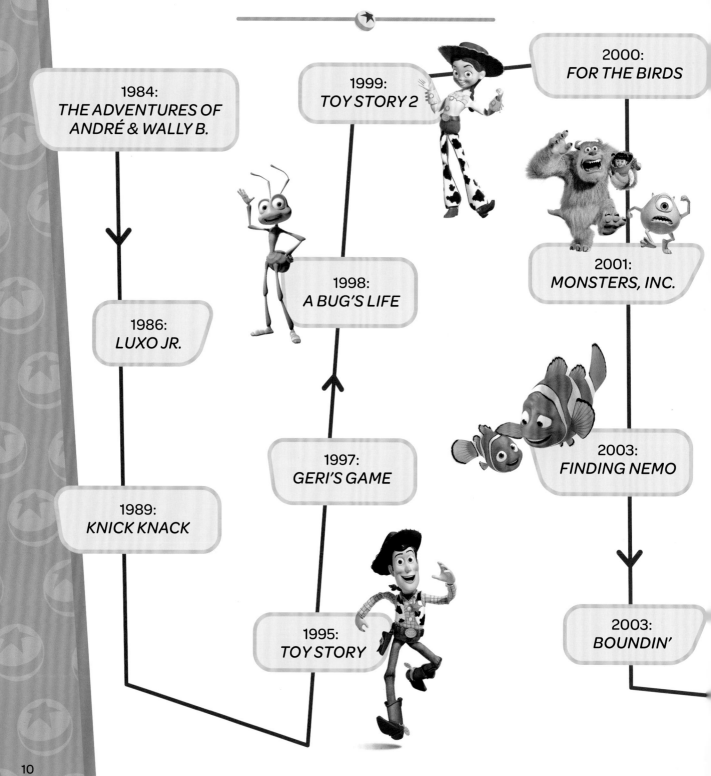

1984:
THE ADVENTURES OF ANDRÉ & WALLY B.

1986:
LUXO JR.

1989:
KNICK KNACK

1995:
TOY STORY

1997:
GERI'S GAME

1998:
A BUG'S LIFE

1999:
TOY STORY 2

2000:
FOR THE BIRDS

2001:
MONSTERS, INC.

2003:
FINDING NEMO

2003:
BOUNDIN'

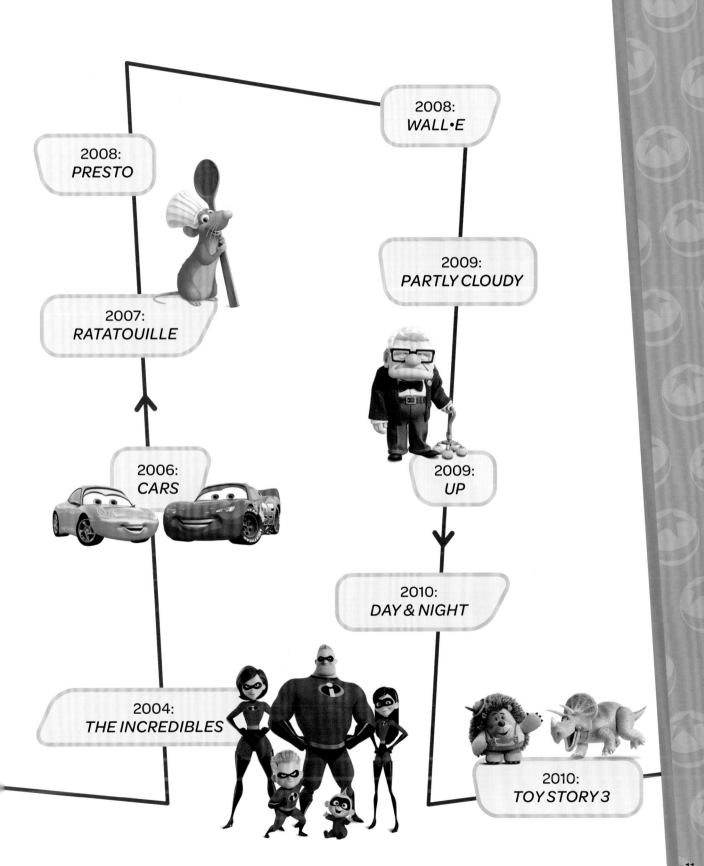

2008:
WALL•E

2008:
PRESTO

2007:
RATATOUILLE

2009:
PARTLY CLOUDY

2006:
CARS

2009:
UP

2010:
DAY & NIGHT

2004:
THE INCREDIBLES

2010:
TOY STORY 3

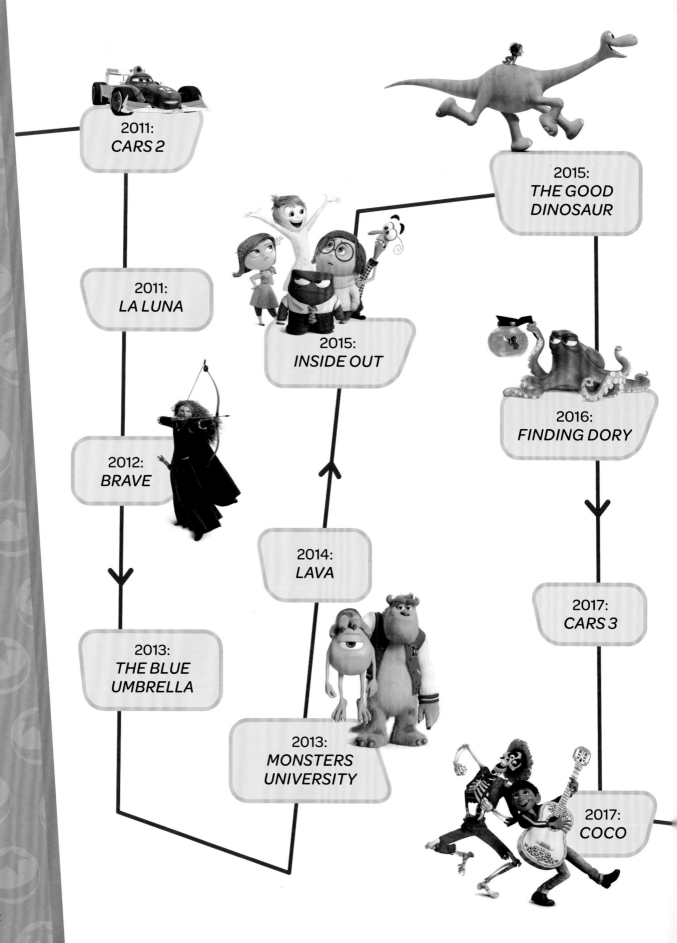

2011:
CARS 2

2015:
THE GOOD DINOSAUR

2011:
LA LUNA

2015:
INSIDE OUT

2016:
FINDING DORY

2012:
BRAVE

2014:
LAVA

2013:
THE BLUE UMBRELLA

2017:
CARS 3

2013:
MONSTERS UNIVERSITY

2017:
COCO

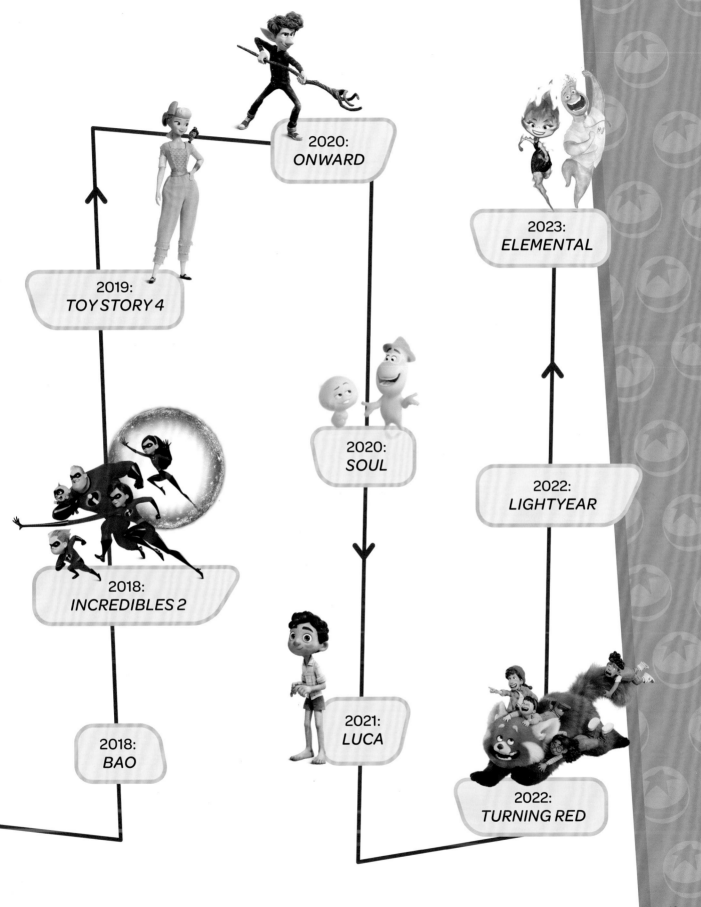

2020:
ONWARD

2023:
ELEMENTAL

2019:
TOY STORY 4

2020:
SOUL

2022:
LIGHTYEAR

2018:
INCREDIBLES 2

2021:
LUCA

2018:
BAO

2022:
TURNING RED

CHAPTER ONE

THE EARLY YEARS

---★---

1984-1999

BEE STINGS

Dessert | YIELD: About 20 donuts | Vegetarian

When the curious André takes a walk through the forest, he encounters the business end of a bee firsthand. And although he might have a thing or two to say about fear, even André would jump at the chance to enjoy these particular Bee Stings. Honey-flavored donut holes are molded into the shape of stingers, creating a tasty tribute to Pixar's very first animated short. Soft, sugary, and packed with a powerfully sweet punch, Bee Stings are sure to make even the most stinger-averse diner *bee* happy.

DOUGH:

1 packet active dry yeast (2¼ teaspoons)

2 tablespoons warm water

1 cup warm milk

¼ cup unsalted butter

2 tablespoons granulated sugar

1 teaspoon salt

½ teaspoon ground cinnamon

3½ cups all-purpose flour, plus more for flouring surface

3 egg yolks

Vegetable oil for frying, plus additional for dipping spoon

TOPPINGS:

¾ cup honey

1 tablespoon water

2 teaspoons cinnamon sugar

TO MAKE THE DOUGH:

Mix the yeast and warm water together and let sit for 5 minutes in the bowl of a stand mixer.

Heat the milk and butter together until the butter has just melted; set aside to cool for 5 minutes.

Mix the yeast mixture, sugar, salt, cinnamon, and 2 cups of flour in the mixer. Add the butter/milk mixture and the eggs.

Slowly mix in the remaining 1½ cups flour, ½ cup at a time, until it forms a dough. Mix for 3 minutes until the dough is fully combined and soft.

Cover the mixing bowl and let rise for 90 minutes or until doubled in size.

Move the dough to a floured surface and use a rolling pin to roll the dough to an even ½-inch thickness.

Using a knife, cut stinger shapes (a rectangle that's rounded on one end and with a pointed tip on the other) approximately 2 inches long.

Cover the stingers with a clean kitchen towel and let rise for 30 more minutes.

TO MAKE THE TOPPINGS:

Once you're about ready to start frying, heat the honey and water in a small saucepan over medium-high heat for 5 minutes. Turn off the heat and let syrup cool slightly while frying the dough.

Place enough oil to fill a large pot 2½ inches deep and heat to 350°F.

Place a couple donuts in the oil at a time, being sure not to let them touch or crowd. Fry each donut until puffed and golden brown, about 1 minute on each side. Place fried donuts on a large plate or baking sheet covered in paper towels to drain.

Move the donuts to a large plate and cover them with the honey syrup. Sprinkle cinnamon sugar over the top and serve warm.

Luxo Jr., 1986

LUXO JR. BALL SLICE AND BAKE COOKIES

Dessert | YIELD: 24 cookies | Vegetarian

For the curious lamp Luxo Jr., there's a whole world just waiting to be discovered. When his father introduces him to a blue-and-yellow ball with a cheerful red star, the toy becomes an instant—albeit short-lived—amusement. These cookies, designed in the colors of the iconic ball, are a playful treat that pairs perfectly with an afternoon spent exploring. With starry, red centers and those instantly recognizable yellow and blue circles, Luxo Jr. Ball Slice and Bake Cookies are a nostalgic nod to a true Pixar icon.

1 cup granulated sugar

1 cup unsalted butter

1 egg

1 teaspoon vanilla

3 cups all-purpose flour

2 teaspoons baking powder

½ teaspoon kosher salt

Yellow, red, and blue gel food coloring

SPECIAL TOOLS NEEDED:

1-inch star-shaped cookie cutter

Mix the sugar and butter in the bowl of a stand mixer until it is light and creamy, scraping down the bowl halfway through.

Add in the egg and vanilla, mixing fully between each addition.

Mix the flour, baking powder, and salt together in a medium bowl, and then slowly add into the butter mixture until everything is fully mixed.

Divide the dough into three separate small bowls.

Place a couple drops of gel food coloring into each bowl (one yellow, one red, and one blue) and mix with the dough until it reaches your desired color. (You may want to wear gloves to prevent your hands from staining!)

Roll out the red dough and use a small star-shaped cookie cutter to cut it into star shapes. Stack the stars together into a long star-shaped log. Use the yellow dough to fill in the crevices, making the log into a cylinder. Roll out the blue dough and wrap it around the cylinder. Wrap with plastic wrap and refrigerate for at least 1 hour.

Preheat the oven to 350°F and line two baking sheets with parchment paper.

Slice the log into ½-inch rounds and place on the baking sheets. Bake for 8 to 10 minutes or until set and barely golden on the edges. Let cool on the baking sheets for 5 minutes and then transfer to a wire rack to cool completely.

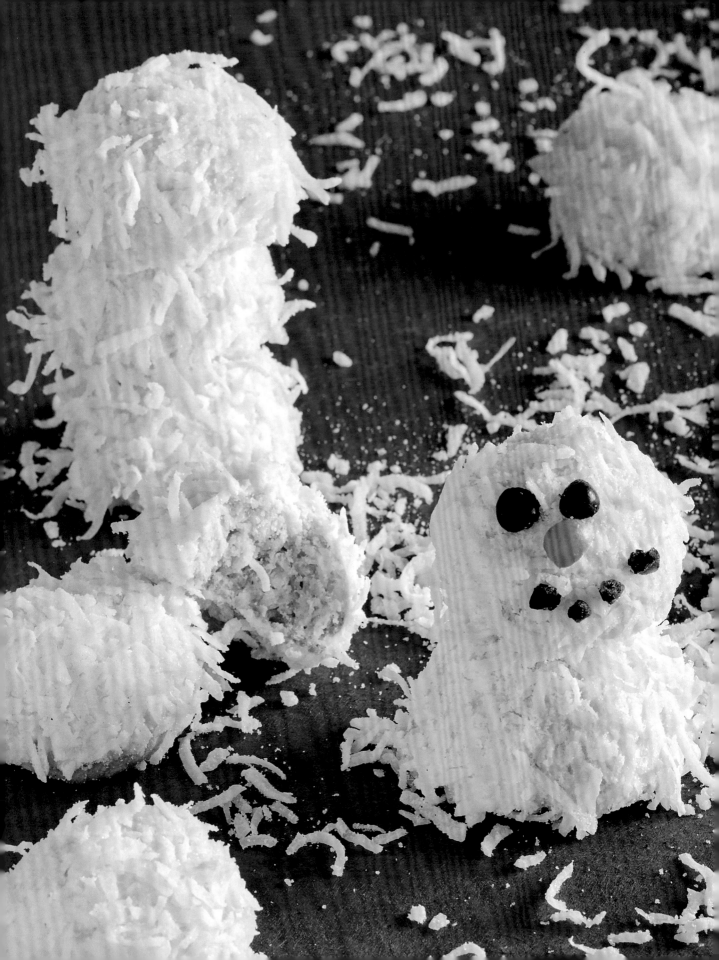

Knick Knack, 1989

SHREDDED COCONUT SNOWBALL COOKIES

Dessert | YIELD: 12 cookies | Vegetarian

Life in a snow globe can be a little isolating. But one entrepreneurial snowman will stop at nothing to make his great escape . . . and to find his perfect match. Inspired by *Knick Knack*'s exceedingly determined hero, Shredded Coconut Snowball Cookies are as charming as they are delicious. Coconut-infused flour is baked into a crumbly cookie ball, then topped with white chocolate candy melts and dipped in coconut flakes. This adorable dessert is bound to be a hit wherever it's served—be it Nome, Alaska; sunny Miami; or even Atlantis!

1 cup sweetened flaked coconut, divided

1 cup all-purpose flour

¼ cup powdered sugar

Pinch of salt

½ cup unsalted butter, softened

1 teaspoon vanilla

8 ounces white chocolate candy melts (or white chocolate chips)

SPECIAL TOOLS NEEDED:

Food processor

Preheat the oven to 350°F and line a baking sheet with parchment paper.

Grind ½ cup flaked coconut in a food processor until it's a fine grain.

Combine the ground coconut, flour, powdered sugar, and salt in the bowl of a stand mixer.

Add the butter and vanilla and mix until the dough comes together.

Roll the dough into 1-inch balls and place 1 inch apart on the baking sheet.

Bake the cookies for 15 minutes—they will have firmed up slightly but won't be too brown.

Let cookies cool completely on a wire rack (at least 15 minutes).

Place the white chocolate candy melts in a bowl and melt in a microwave according to directions (or melt white chocolate chips in a microwave for 30 seconds at a time, stirring between each interval). Place the remaining ½ cup shredded coconut on a plate.

Dip the top of each cookie in the melted chocolate and then dip in the coconut. Let cool until the chocolate is hardened.

FUN FACT

The snow globe from the short film *Knick Knack* is one of the items that can be found in WALL·E's trailer and the trash on Earth.

MOVIE SPOTLIGHT:
TOY STORY

Memorable Quote: "To infinity and beyond!"

Release Years: *Toy Story* (1995), *Toy Story 2* (1999),
Toy Story 3 (2010), *Toy Story 4* (2019)

Director: John Lasseter (*Toy Story*, *Toy Story 2*),
Lee Unkrich (*Toy Story 3*), Josh Cooley (*Toy Story 4*)

In *Toy Story*, Pixar answers the question every child asks: Do toys come to life when people aren't around? When Andy's favorite toy cowboy, Woody, feels threatened by the arrival of a fearless Space Ranger, he worries he'll lose his place in Andy's heart. But when Woody and Buzz Lightyear find themselves trapped inside the home of a toy-destroying child named Sid, they must work together to make their way back to Andy before they are lost to him forever. Packed with emotion and filled with adventures befitting toys, kids, and kids at heart, *Toy Story* takes audiences on a play-packed journey to infinity and beyond.

But any good journey requires a solid dose of sustenance. And in *Toy Story,* food fuels the storyline, powering Andy and his friends through their out-of-the ordinary adventures. It's also a means through which the characters can forge meaningful connections with the people—and toys—they've chosen to love. In *Toy Story*, Andy is overjoyed when his mom asks, "What would you say to dinner at uh, oh, Pizza Planet?" The popular restaurant is a place where mother and son can make happy memories together, marvel at the aliens in the claw machine, and of course, share their thoughts about their upcoming move. In *Toy Story 3*, Bonnie hosts a heartwarming welcome party for Andy's memorable, now hand-me-down toy, Woody. She gives the cowboy a seat at her play table, where he's introduced to Mr. Pricklepants, Buttercup, and Trixie. There, the toys connect over cups of imaginary coffee and marvel at the fact that Bonnie's hamburger is topped with a secret ingredient— jelly beans! And in *Toy Story 4,* Bonnie goes off to school and makes a new friend (literally!) when she constructs her memorable Forky using an eating utensil! For both Andy and Bonnie, food is a hallmark of key family moments—from leaving a childhood home to introducing new friends to old. And in the world of *Toy Story*, shared meals are important— and joyful—points of connection . . . so long as nobody's poisoned the well!

One of *Toy Story*'s most iconic food-related images—the Pizza Planet delivery truck— has been featured in nearly every Pixar film. Because the *Toy Story* movies span the course of Andy's childhood, Pixar animators gave the Pizza Planet truck different looks in each film. Its degree of rust, dust, and weathering offered viewers a visual nod to the passage of time.

Although the toys' four films spanned twelve years of Andy's life (and twenty-four years of Pixar's!), the movies retained many of their animators over the course of their production. Seventeen original *Toy Story* animators went on to work on *Toy Story 2,* and four worked on three of the films. When *Toy Story 3* wrapped, the film's director led a thrilling march through Pixar's Emeryville studio. Lee Unkrich was accompanied by two snare drummers, two bass drummers, two giant monkeys, and one yeti. One can only imagine that this highly entertaining send-off was delivered amid much laughter, a few nostalgic tears, and perhaps even a shared, celebratory meal. Pizza Planet, anyone?

Toy Story, 1995

PIZZA PLANET PIZZA

Entrée | YIELD: 1 large pizza | Vegetarian

Pizza Planet is Andy's favorite restaurant for a reason. Not only does it have amazing pizza to eat and countless games to play, it's also designed to look like a real galactic space station—the home of Andy's newest (and most exciting!) toy, Buzz Lightyear. Pizza Planet Pizza is a classic pizza dish that evokes all the flavors of Andy's go-to treat. With five types of cheese and a vast array of seasonings, this recipe will have diners reaching for another slice—no claw required. Next stop, Pizza Planet!

PIZZA DOUGH:

1 cup warm water

1 tablespoon honey

2 teaspoons active dry yeast

3 cups all-purpose flour, plus more for dusting

½ teaspoon kosher salt

1 tablespoon olive oil, plus more for bowl

SAUCE:

One 15-ounce can tomato sauce

¼ cup water

1 teaspoon granulated sugar

¼ teaspoon dried basil

¼ teaspoon dried oregano

¼ teaspoon dried thyme

¼ teaspoon garlic powder

¼ teaspoon kosher salt

Dash of freshly ground black pepper

TO MAKE THE PIZZA DOUGH:

Place the water, honey, and yeast into the bowl of a stand mixer fitted with a dough hook and let rest for 10 minutes, or until the yeast begins to froth.

Add the flour, salt, and olive oil to the bowl and mix for 10 minutes or until dough is firm and elastic.

Place the dough into an oiled bowl, cover with a damp towel, and let rise for 45 minutes or until dough doubles in size.

TO MAKE THE SAUCE:

Mix the tomato sauce, water, sugar, basil, oregano, thyme, garlic powder, salt, and pepper together in a small saucepan and cook, covered, over medium heat until it starts to boil (about 1 to 2 minutes). Lower the heat and simmer for 30 minutes. Cool in the refrigerator until room temperature. (You'll only use half the sauce for this recipe.)

TOPPINGS:

⅓ cup cheddar cheese, freshly shredded

⅓ cup fresh mozzarella, freshly shredded

⅓ cup provolone cheese, freshly shredded

⅓ cup Gouda cheese, freshly shredded

⅓ cup Parmesan cheese, freshly shredded

SPECIAL TOOLS NEEDED:

Pizza pan (or large baking sheet)

Cutting board

Pizza cutter, mezzaluna, or large knife

TO MAKE THE PIZZA:

Preheat the oven to 450°F and oil a pizza pan or baking sheet.

With floured hands, punch the pizza dough down and form a disc. Slowly stretch the dough into a large circle by holding one edge and continuing to rotate along the edge, letting gravity stretch it downwards. Continue until the pizza crust is 12 to 14 inches in diameter and even in thickness. Place onto the pizza pan or baking sheet.

Place ½ cup of sauce in the middle of the pizza crust and use the back of a spoon to lightly spread it around the rest of the crust, leaving a ½-inch border around the edge. Mix the cheddar, mozzarella, provolone, Gouda, and Parmesan cheeses together and sprinkle evenly on top of the sauce.

Bake for 12 to 15 minutes, or until the crust is golden and the cheese is melted and beginning to brown.

Remove the pizza from the oven and transfer onto a cutting board. Let sit for a few minutes and cut into 8 pieces.

FUN FACT

No motion-capture is used in the entire *Toy Story* film—everything is animated by hand.

Toy Story, 1995

HOWDY HOT DOGS

Entrée | YIELD: 4 dogs | Dairy Free

Slinky Dog is one of Andy's favorite toys and a loyal friend to Woody. With his canine-shaped ends and metallic, swirling center, he offers hours of entertainment. But his namesake dish won't last nearly that long—in fact, it'll be gobbled off the plate faster than you can say, "Golly bob howdy!" After all, a spiraled hot dog is just too fun to resist.

4 hot dogs

4 hot dog buns

¼ cup jalapeño slices

¼ yellow onion, sliced

SPECIAL TOOLS NEEDED:

4 skewers (if wooden, soak in water for 30 minutes)

Grill

Preheat the grill to medium-high heat.

Place each hot dog on a skewer and then place on a cutting board.

Spiral cut each hot dog by taking a paring knife and, starting ¼ inch from the end of the hot dog, cutting into the dog at an angle. Rotate the dog, moving the knife in one continuous cut at the same angle until you reach the other end.

Carefully pull the spiral-cut dog apart slightly, giving some room between the spirals on the skewer.

Continue with the other three hot dogs.

Grill the dogs for 5 minutes, turning occasionally for an even cook.

Remove from the skewers and place each dog in a hot dog bun, topping it with jalapeño slices (to represent Slinky's collar) and onion slices (to represent his coils), and condiments of your choice.

FUN FACT

Toy Story was created using the smallest animation staff for a Disney animation feature.

Toy Story, 1995

SUPERNOVA BURGERS

Entrée | YIELD: 3 burgers

When Buzz Lightyear seemingly drops in from the sky, Woody's convinced that his world has come to an end. But he quickly realizes that he's got a friend in Buzz—one whose tastes just happen to be out of this world! The Supernova Burger is a fun twist on a classic hamburger. With cheese, onion rings, and a special Supernova Sauce, this recipe serves up an exquisite explosion of flavor . . . no space travel required!

SUPERNOVA SAUCE:

¼ cup mayonnaise

2 tablespoons ketchup

1 teaspoon relish

1 teaspoon granulated sugar

1 teaspoon white vinegar

½ teaspoon freshly ground black pepper

½ teaspoon paprika

¼ teaspoon garlic powder

¼ teaspoon onion powder

BATTERED ONION RINGS:

Canola oil, for frying

1 sweet onion (or yellow onion if unable to find sweet)

2 tablespoons cornstarch

1 cup buttermilk

¾ cup all-purpose flour

½ teaspoon kosher salt

¼ teaspoon freshly ground black pepper

¼ teaspoon cayenne pepper

TO MAKE THE SUPERNOVA SAUCE:

In a small bowl, mix the mayonnaise, ketchup, relish, sugar, vinegar, pepper, paprika, garlic powder, and onion powder, then store in the refrigerator until ready to use.

TO MAKE THE ONION RINGS:

Place canola oil in a Dutch oven or heavy pot until it covers at least 1 inch of the bottom. Heat on medium-high heat until oil reaches a temperature of 375°F. Slice the sweet onion into rings. Place the cornstarch on a plate, then dip each onion ring into the cornstarch. Mix the buttermilk, flour, salt, pepper, and cayenne pepper in a medium bowl, and dip the cornstarch-covered onion rings into the batter. Fry the battered onion rings in the oil for 4 to 5 minutes, turning over halfway, until golden brown and crisp. Remove with tongs and place on a paper towel–lined plate.

TO PREPARE THE TOPPINGS:

Preheat a griddle or a cast-iron pan on high heat. Butter the inside of each bun and give them a quick toast on the griddle or pan while it's preheating. Set the buns on two plates. Spread the Supernova Sauce on the inside of the buns and prep the bottom bun with lettuce and pickle slices. Place two battered onion rings on the top bun.

TOPPINGS:

3 brioche buns, split

1 tablespoon salted butter

½ cup shredded lettuce

9 pickle slices

3 slices American cheese

BURGER PATTIES:

1 pound 80/20 ground beef

1 teaspoon salt

½ teaspoon freshly ground black pepper

TO MAKE THE BURGER PATTIES:

Mix the ground beef, salt, and black pepper in a medium bowl and divide the beef mixture into six equal pieces. Roll the beef into loose balls.

Place one of the balls onto the hot griddle or pan and smash it down to a thin patty with a stiff spatula. Cook for 45 seconds and then scrape it up and flip it. Cook for another minute or until browned with crispy edges. Continue with the rest of the patties.

Place one patty on each bottom bun, then top with a slice of American cheese and the other patty. Place the onion rings and top bun on top. Serve with additional onion rings and additional Supernova Sauce on the side for dipping the rings.

FUN FACT

The most complicated animation shot in *Toy Story* was of the army men attacking Woody. To get a feel for how army men would walk on solid bases, animators nailed a pair of shoes to a piece of plywood and hopped around.

Toy Story, 1995

ALIEN SLIME SODA

Drink | YIELD: 1 serving | Vegetarian, Vegan, Dairy Free, Gluten Free

Those little green aliens trapped in a claw machine inside Andy's beloved Pizza Planet have an otherworldly reverence for The Claw. It drops from the sky, selecting one lucky creature for a trip to parts unknown. But waiting to be chosen can be tiresome . . . and could be made more palatable with the addition of a fun, fizzy beverage. With its lemon-lime flavors and shocking green hue, Alien Slime Soda is just the thing to serve when waiting on your next alien invasion . . . or hosting a gaggle of guests—green or otherwise!

3 ounces simple syrup

1 ounce lemon juice

1 ounce lime juice

4 drops green food coloring

2 drops yellow food coloring

7 ounces club soda

In a tall glass, mix the simple syrup, lemon juice, lime juice, and food coloring.

Add the club soda and stir gently to combine until the entire drink is neon green.

Geri's Game, 1997

CHESSBOARD COOKIES

Dessert | YIELD: 45 cookies | Vegetarian

It's been said that one doesn't play the game of chess, one plays their opponent. But for the octogenarian Geri, life is always about outwitting himself. Chessboard Cookies memorialize that famous day in the park when Geri battled fiercely—in every way he knew how. Made with cocoa powder and vanilla squares that mimic the pattern of Geri's beloved board, Chessboard Cookies are the perfect way to wind down after a day of playing games. And should sharing these beloved cookies prove to be too difficult, there's always Geri's tried-and-true gambit . . . hiding his opponent's dentures!

1 cup salted butter, softened

1 cup granulated sugar

1 egg, plus 1 egg yolk

1 teaspoon vanilla

3 cups all-purpose flour

1½ teaspoons baking powder

½ teaspoon kosher salt

⅓ cup black cocoa powder

FUN FACT

The cleaner who comes to repair Woody in *Toy Story 2* is Geri. His toolbox even has a drawer full of chess pieces.

Cream the butter and sugar together in the bowl of a stand mixer for 2 minutes or until even and light.

Add in the egg, yolk, and vanilla and mix until smooth.

In a medium bowl, combine the flour, baking powder, and salt.

Add the flour mixture to the butter mixture slowly, mixing until just combined.

Split the dough in two, removing one half from the bowl. Add the black cocoa powder to the remaining dough and mix until evenly combined.

Roll each dough into a log about 6 inches long and press down on each side to turn the circular log into a rectangular shape with square sides. Make sure both square logs are the same size and shape. Wrap dough in plastic wrap and refrigerate for 1 hour.

Remove each dough log and cut each log into 3 equal-sized strips lengthwise. Rotate the logs and cut into thirds again, resulting in 9 equal-sized strips.

Now it's time to make the "chessboard." Lay one vanilla strip, then one chocolate strip, then another vanilla strip next to each other. Top these strips with the alternating colors (chocolate, vanilla, chocolate), and then top once again with the same colors as the first row. Press the dough together to make a tight square, then wrap in plastic wrap and refrigerate for another 30 minutes.

Repeat with the other set of dough.

While the dough chills, preheat the oven to 350°F and line a large baking sheet with parchment paper.

Slice the chilled dough logs into ¼-inch-thick cookies and place on the baking sheet.

Bake for 9 to 10 minutes or until firm and just beginning to brown. Cool on a wire rack.

A Bug's Life, 1998

BUGGY PLATTER

Appetizer | YIELD: 12 wontons | Vegetarian

When the adventurous ant Flik walks into a bug bar, he discovers that the local offerings aren't exactly to his liking. While the local flies swarm to devour their much-loved "poo poo platter," the finicky Flik is significantly less impressed. But as any host knows, feeding a crowd requires some creativity. And a pupu platter is the perfect way to offer a bevy of treats on one artistic plate. Fried wontons are a traditional item on any proper platter, and this recipe offers a fun twist on a well-known party dish. Refried beans, cheddar cheese, and a dash of chili powder make these wontons extra tasty. And with a few adjustments, this platter might grow big enough to serve the entire colony . . . and oppressed ants everywhere!

¾ cup canned refried beans

⅓ cup shredded cheddar cheese

½ teaspoon cumin

Dash of chili powder

12 wonton wrappers

4 cups canola oil (or enough to coat bottom 1 inch of pan)

In a small bowl, mix the beans, cheese, cumin, and chili powder.

Place the wonton wrappers on a flat surface, and place 1 tablespoon of bean mixture into the middle of each wrapper.

Wet your fingers and fold over the edges of the wonton wrapper, wrapping a bit like a burrito.

Fill a medium-large pot with canola oil, coating the bottom inch of the pot. Heat to 375°F and place the wontons in the pot, not allowing them to touch or be too crowded. (You may need to do multiple batches.)

Fry for 3 to 5 minutes, turning over halfway, until the wontons are golden brown and slightly bubbly looking.

Place the fried wontons on a paper towel–lined plate to drain.

FUN FACT

The dog collar on a table at the yard sale in *Toy Story 2* originally appeared as the center ring in P.T. Flea's Circus in *A Bug's Life.*

A Bug's Life, 1998

HEIMLICH'S BOYSENBERRY PIES

Dessert | YIELD: 6 pies | Vegetarian

The rotund caterpillar Heimlich hates performing on an empty stomach. He does his best work when his belly is filled with sweets—from watermelon to his beloved candy corn. Because Heimlich works so hard—both in the circus and at becoming a beautiful butterfly—he deserves the occasional treat. And this boysenberry mini pie is just the thing to tide over a very hungry caterpillar. It may be tough to be a bug . . . but it can have its perks, too!

PIE CRUST:

1¼ cups all-purpose flour

½ teaspoon kosher salt

½ tablespoons granulated sugar

½ cup unsalted butter, cold and diced

¼ cup cold water

1 egg

FILLING:

3 cups boysenberries

¼ cup granulated sugar

2 tablespoons orange juice

1 tablespoon cornstarch

½ teaspoon vanilla

SPECIAL TOOLS NEEDED:

Muffin tin

4-inch biscuit cutter

TO MAKE THE PIE CRUST:

Mix the flour, salt, and sugar together in a large bowl.

Place the butter cubes in the bowl with the flour mixture, and using your hands, squeeze and mix everything together until fully mixed and slightly crumbly.

Sprinkle some of the water over the dough mixture and mix until the dough fully sticks together. If it's still crumbly, add a bit more water.

Form into a ball and then press into a disc. Wrap in plastic wrap and refrigerate for 1 hour.

Flour a large surface and roll the dough out with a rolling pin until it's ⅛ inch thick. Cut six rounds with a 4-inch biscuit cutter and place each round into a muffin tin. Cut strips ¼ inch thick from the rest of the dough and set aside.

Preheat the oven to 350°F.

Note:
Limited on time? Use a pre-made (pre-cooked) pie crust and skip to step 6.

Boysenberries not in season? Substitute raspberries, blackberries, blueberries, or a berry mixture.

TO MAKE THE FILLING:

In a medium pot, mix the boysenberries, sugar, orange juice, and cornstarch together and bring to a boil over medium heat. Reduce heat to low and let simmer once it begins boiling. Cook for 5 minutes, or until the boysenberries have softened and the mixture has thickened. Add the vanilla and mix. Remove from the stove and let cool.

Place 2 tablespoons filling in each prepared pie crust, and then top with the strips of dough in a loose weave. (You will have some leftover filling. Try it over ice cream—it's delicious!)

Whisk the egg with 1 teaspoon water and brush the egg wash over the pie crusts.

Bake for 20 to 25 minutes, or until the pie crusts are golden and the filling is bubbling.

Move to a wire rack and let cool.

FUN FACT

On the toys' journey to Al's Toy Barn in *Toy Story 2*, Buzz chops through some shrubs. If you look closely, you can see Heimlich from *A Bug's Life* climbing a branch.

CHAPTER TWO
THE NEXT GENERATION

2000-2009

FOR THE BIRDS SEED

Snack | **YIELD:** 6 cups granola | Vegetarian, Dairy Free, Gluten Free

It's tough to be a bird. There are cats to avoid, long migrations to fly, and meals to procure. And of course, there's that tricky social hierarchy that all flocks must eventually navigate. This recipe offers a fun nod to our avian friends—and their not-always-so-friendly adventures high atop a roadside power line. *For the Birds* Seed combines bird-friendly ingredients such as oats, seeds, and almond butter into a homemade granola mix that can be both sweet and salty . . . just like the flocks themselves.

3 cups old-fashioned rolled oats

1 cup sliced almonds

½ cup shelled sunflower seeds

2 tablespoons flax seed

2 tablespoons sesame seeds

⅓ cup coconut oil

½ cup honey

3 tablespoons almond butter

1 teaspoon cinnamon

½ teaspoon kosher salt

1 cup dried cherries

Preheat the oven to 300°F and line a large rimmed baking sheet with parchment paper.

Combine the oats, almonds, and sunflower, flax, and sesame seeds in a large bowl.

Place the coconut oil, honey, and almond butter in a small microwave-safe bowl and microwave for 30 seconds. Add the cinnamon and kosher salt and stir together.

Pour the melted mixture over the dry ingredients and mix until evenly coated.

Spread the granola mixture onto the baking sheet in an even layer. If you want more clumps in your granola, use your hands to bunch up the granola on the baking sheet.

Bake for 20 minutes, stirring halfway. The granola will be done when lightly browned and mostly dried.

Once out of the oven, let cool completely (about 45 minutes) and then mix in the dried cherries. Transfer to an airtight container, where the granola can stay at room temperature for up to a month.

Monsters, Inc., 2001

KREATURE KRISPS

Snack | YIELD: 8 cups snack mix | Vegetarian

The Scarers at Monsters Incorporated know that success begins with a few simple ingredients: hard work, sharp teeth, and of course, a hearty snack. After all, nobody can do their best work on an empty stomach . . . even one that emits a menacing growl! Kreature Krisps offer the perfect way for monsters of all ages to start their day. Packed with oat circles, nuts, and pretzel rods, Kreature Krisps are sure to earn screams of approval from even the mightiest little scarer.

3 tablespoons salted butter

1 tablespoon Worcestershire sauce

¼ teaspoon garlic powder

¼ teaspoon onion powder

¼ teaspoon kosher salt

Dash of paprika

4 cups toasted oat circles cereal

1 cup mixed nuts

1 cup mini pretzel rods

1 cup cheese crackers

1 cup oyster crackers

Preheat the oven to 250°F and line a large rimmed baking sheet with parchment paper.

Melt the butter in a large bowl in the microwave for 30 seconds. Stir, and microwave again until melted.

Mix the Worcestershire sauce, garlic powder, onion powder, salt, and paprika into the butter.

Place the cereal, nuts, pretzels, cheese crackers, and oyster crackers into a large bowl or zippered bag. Drizzle the sauce over the top and toss the cereal mixture until everything is evenly coated. Pour out onto the baking sheet and bake for 20 minutes, stirring halfway through.

Let cool and then serve or store in an airtight container for up to 1 week.

FUN FACT

At the start of *Monsters, Inc.*, the team at Pixar commissioned their favorite children's book illustrators to do inspirational designs for Monstropolis. The illustrators were given total design freedom, and the team used their unique, inspirational designs to successfully produce the parallel universe in which the Scarers at Monsters Incorporated live.

SCREAM FACTORY HOT WINGS

Appetizer | YIELD: 2 servings (1 pound of chicken wings each) | Gluten Free

Before it switched over to running on laugh power, the city of Monstropolis operated on scream energy. This clean, mean power source was a highly efficient way to run absolutely everything within the city . . . and it was easily acquired by the energetic team at Monsters, Inc. But had those scream canisters ever run low, this frighteningly hot, perfectly peppered poultry dish would have been sure to top them off. After all, if seeing a ghost is cause for alarm . . . then just imagine eating one . . . in pepper form!

CHICKEN WINGS:

1 tablespoon baking powder

1 teaspoon garlic powder

1 teaspoon kosher salt

½ teaspoon freshly ground black pepper

½ teaspoon smoked paprika

2 pounds chicken wings, separated and wing tips removed

Celery, blue cheese dressing, and milk, for serving (optional)

SAUCE:

¼ cup salted butter

½ cup medium-hot hot sauce

1 teaspoon ghost pepper powder or sauce

TO MAKE THE CHICKEN WINGS:

Preheat the oven to 400°F and line a large baking sheet with parchment paper or a rack.

Mix the baking powder, garlic powder, salt, pepper, and smoked paprika in a large bowl. Set aside.

Pat the chicken wings dry with a paper towel. Place the chicken wings in the bowl of seasoning and toss to coat. Place the seasoned chicken wings on the baking sheet.

Cook for 50 minutes, turning them over halfway through, and prepare the sauce while cooking.

TO PREPARE THE SAUCE:

In a small saucepan, melt the butter on low heat. Add the hot sauce and ghost pepper powder. Whisk carefully until well combined. Place the sauce into a large bowl.

Once the chicken is browned and crispy, remove from the oven and toss the wings with the sauce. (You may want to wear gloves/goggles for this to protect your hands and eyes from the spices.)

Serve with celery sticks, blue cheese dressing, and milk for those who can't take the heat!

FUN FACT

The animators recognized that there were almost limitless design possibilities when creating the monsters who inhabit Monstropolis. Designers found inspiration in both real animals and what children imagined monsters looked like.

HARRYHAUSEN'S SUSHI

Entrée | YIELD: 12 rice balls

It's practically impossible to get a reservation at Harryhausen's. But Mike "Googly Bear" Wazowski will stop at nothing to give his girlfriend Celia the perfect birthday surprise. The restaurant is known for its delicate sushi rolls—and its elegant, ginger-scented dining room. And this unique take on Harryhausen's Sushi evokes all eyeball-shaped delicacies seen on the diners' plates at Monstropolis's most famous restaurant, without the danger of encountering a 2319. Just be sure to avoid any human children wandering among the tables. After all, the CDA is always watching . . .

2 cups sushi rice

3 cups water

1 tablespoon salted butter

1 salmon fillet, skin removed

Dash of salt and pepper

1 tablespoon soy sauce

½ teaspoon sesame oil

4 black olives

Rinse the rice until the water comes out clear.

Place the rice and the water in a large pot over medium-high heat and bring to a boil. Reduce heat to low, cover, and cook for 20 minutes, or until the water is absorbed. Remove from the heat and set aside to cool.

While the rice is cooking, heat the butter in a medium skillet over medium heat, and add the salmon fillet. Sprinkle a dash of salt and pepper on the top of the salmon. Cook for 4 minutes on one side, flip, and cook for 3 minutes longer, or until salmon feels firm to the touch. Break the salmon up into small flakes, add the soy sauce, and continue to cook until the sauce is fully incorporated. Remove from heat.

Mix half of the salmon with the rice and sesame oil.

Wet your hands, then take a handful of rice and mold it into a ball, approximately 1½ inches in diameter. Wet your hands again between each ball.

Slice each black olive into three circular slices, and place one on the middle of each ball.

Serve your rice (eye) balls to the fanciest clientele—no children allowed!

Monsters, Inc., 2001

ABOMINABLE SNOW CONES

Dessert | YIELD: 8 snow cones | Vegetarian, Vegan, Dairy Free, Gluten Free

When Mike and Sulley uncover a nefarious workplace plot, they're thrown into a cover-up of monstrous proportions. They're immediately banished to the Himalayas, where Sulley nearly freezes his fur off! There they meet the Abominable Snowman, who may seem ferocious at first but turns out to be more Adorable than Abominable. He teaches Mike and Sulley that when life hands you lemons, you make lemon snow cones. With sugar, water, and just a splash of lemon juice, this refreshing recipe would make the Abominable Snowman proud. Welcome to the Himalayas!

2 cups granulated sugar

1 cup water

¼ cup lemon juice (about 1 large lemon)

5 drops yellow food coloring

8 cups ice

SPECIAL TOOLS NEEDED:

Snow-cone machine or blender

Place the sugar and water in a small pan and heat over medium heat, stirring often, until the sugar has dissolved and the mixture has formed a simple syrup, about 3 minutes.

Remove the syrup from heat and stir in the lemon juice and the yellow food coloring. Refrigerate the syrup until chilled, about 2 hours.

Crush the ice: If you have access to a snow-cone machine, use that. Otherwise, pulse the ice in a blender until it's finely crushed.

Pack the crushed ice into paper cones or in a bowl. Drizzle about ¼ cup syrup onto each snow cone and serve.

Monsters, Inc., 2001

SLUDGE COFFEE

Drink | YIELD: 1 serving | Vegetarian, Vegan, Gluten Free

Mornings in Monstropolis can be rough for monsters. After all, it's hard to roll out of bed when you have nine arms! Luckily for Sulley, the ever-cheerful Mike Wazowski is always ready with a hot cup of sludge. It's just the kick in the fur he needs to get out of bed, warm up his scary feet, and venture onto the Scare Floor. And with sugar, chocolate, and plenty of coffee, this sludge-inspired smoothie is strong enough to power even the most sluggish scarer . . . a monstrously impressive feat!

¾ cup coffee, cooled (or cold brew)

½ cup milk of your choice

½ cup vanilla Greek yogurt

1 banana

2 tablespoons dark chocolate syrup

1 teaspoon granulated sugar

1 cup ice cubes

Combine the coffee, milk, Greek yogurt, banana, chocolate syrup, sugar, and ice cubes into a blender and blend for 1 minute until smooth.

Pour into a tall glass and start your day off right.

SPECIAL TOOLS NEEDED:

Blender

NOTHING FISHY VEGETARIAN SUSHI ROLLS

Entrée | YIELD: 30 pieces of sushi | Vegetarian

Bruce works really, really hard in his fish-friendly shark support group. He knows he's not a mindless eating machine . . . though the temptation is definitely there! Luckily for Bruce, he has his buddies to keep him in check. And he can always snack on fish-free treats . . . like these vegetarian sushi rolls. With carrots, avocados, and shredded purple cabbage, Nothing Fishy Vegetarian Sushi Rolls make the perfect snack for any group meeting, after-school treat, or light lunch. After all: "Fish are friends—not food!"

2 cups sushi rice

3 cups water

½ cup rice vinegar

1 tablespoon canola oil

¼ cup plus ½ teaspoon granulated sugar, divided

1 teaspoon kosher salt

5 sheets nori

1 cup shredded purple cabbage

1 large carrot, peeled and julienned

½ cucumber, julienned

1 avocado, sliced thin

⅓ cup mayo

2 teaspoons sriracha (more or less to taste)

1 lime wedge

Soy sauce, for serving

SPECIAL TOOLS NEEDED:

Bamboo sushi mat

Rinse the rice until the water comes out clear.

Place the rice and the water in a large pot over medium-high heat and bring to a boil. Reduce heat to low, cover, and cook for 20 minutes, or until the water is absorbed. Remove from the heat and set aside to cool.

Mix the rice vinegar, oil, ¼ cup sugar, and salt in a small saucepan over medium heat. Cook for about a minute, or until the sugar and salt have dissolved. Remove from heat and let cool for 5 minutes.

Pour the sauce over the rice and mix.

Place a nori sheet rough side up on a bamboo sushi mat.

Wet your hands, then take ¾ cup rice and press it into an even layer on top of the nori, leaving ¼ inch at the top edge without rice.

Place ⅕ of the cabbage, carrot, cucumber, and avocado slices on the first ⅓ of the rice, then use the bamboo mat to tightly roll it up. Moisten the edge of the nori that doesn't contain rice with water to help seal it to the roll.

Cut the roll in 6 pieces, trimming any uneven edges from the rolls.

Repeat with the rest of the rice, nori, and vegetables.

In a small bowl, combine mayo, sriracha, a squeeze of lime juice from the lime wedge, and the remaining ½ teaspoon sugar. Drizzle the spicy mayo over the sushi.

Serve with a side of soy sauce, and remember: Fish are friends, not food!

Finding Nemo, 2003

"MADE ME INK" PASTA

Entrée | YIELD: 4 servings | Vegetarian

Nervous sea creatures have been known to have some rather peculiar traits. One might puff into a spiky ball, while another might shoot out a cloud of ink! But a wise chef knows not to be deterred by a little mess. After all, that "ink" might just be the perfect secret ingredient for a truly delectable pasta sauce! This "Made Me Ink" Pasta is a playful nod to Pearl the Octopus's adorable, nervous habit. Made with eggs, flour, and a special ink-hued ingredient, these homemade noodles are sure to please even the pickiest little guppies!

2 cups 00 flour, plus more for dusting

4 large eggs

1 tablespoon olive oil, plus more for dressing the pasta

½ teaspoon black food coloring

1 teaspoon kosher salt

¼ cup grated Parmesan cheese

On a large cutting board, place the flour into a mound. Make a well in the center and place the eggs, olive oil, food coloring, and salt inside.

Using a fork, beat the egg mixture together, and once combined, slowly start incorporating the flour along the edges of the well. Continue to incorporate until it's completely mixed into a dough.

Knead the dough for 2 to 5 minutes or until it is smooth and firm. If too wet, add more flour 1 teaspoon at a time.

Form the dough into a disc, wrap in plastic wrap, and let rest for 30 minutes.

Once rested, cut the dough into quarters and roll into logs approximately 12 to 14 inches long.

Place one log on a floured surface and roll out the width (keeping the length) very thin (about 1 to 2 millimeters). (If you have a pasta machine, you can use it to help you roll out the pasta and cut it.)

Cut the pasta in thin, long strips to make fettuccine noodles. Repeat steps 6 to 7 with the rest of the dough.

Bring a large pot of salted water to a boil, and cook the pasta until al dente, about 1 to 2 minutes. Drain, and toss with olive oil and Parmesan or use your favorite sauce.

Finding Nemo, 2003

MINE, MINE, MINE CHIPS

Side | YIELD: 1 pound of fries | Dairy Free, Gluten Free

Seagulls love their French fries—or as the birds Down Under call them, chips! These salty fried potatoes will make any self-respecting seagull dive out of the sky and proudly declare, "Mine! Mine! Mine!" And this aptly named dish promises to be a highly sought-after side at the next barbeque, family gathering, or after-school event. Cooked up fresh and seasoned with the popular Aussie spice, chicken salt, Mine, Mine, Mine Chips are sure to be snatched off their serving dish in no time! Just watch out for the 'gulls!

1 pound (about 3) russet potatoes

Vegetable oil, for frying

3 tablespoons chicken salt (or more or less to taste)

SPECIAL TOOLS NEEDED:

Deep pot or Dutch oven for frying

Peel the potatoes and cut them into ½-inch strips. Soak the potato strips in cold water for at least 1 hour, then rinse and pat dry.

Heat 3 inches of vegetable oil in a large, heavy pot to 325°F. Using tongs, place some of the fries into the pot (enough where they are fully submerged and not overcrowded). Cook the fries for 5 to 6 minutes, then remove and set them on a paper towel–lined plate. Continue with all of the fries.

Heat the oil up to 400°F and cook each batch of fries a second time until they are crisp and golden brown (about 2 to 3 minutes). This will help make an extra crispy fry. Set on a paper towel–lined plate, add the chicken salt to taste and plate.

Note:
Want to make your own chicken salt? Combine 6 tablespoons table salt, 3 tablespoons powdered chicken bouillon, 3 tablespoons garlic powder, 3 tablespoons sweet paprika, 1 teaspoon white pepper, 1 teaspoon onion powder, and 1 teaspoon celery seeds.

These fries are coated with chicken salt, an Australian seasoning that can be found on most fast food fries Down Under. You can find regular or vegan varieties at specialty spice shops or online.

FUN FACT

The Pizza Planet truck from *Toy Story* can be seen on the highway near the dentist's office.

Boundin', 2003

BOUNDIN' POPCORN

Snack | YIELD: 5 cups of popcorn | Vegetarian, Gluten Free

The Great American Jackalope is renowned across the prairie for his consummate wisdom. He knows that life comes in waves, but with a healthy dose of perspective—and the willingness to bound for the sky—things will always turn around. *Boundin'* Popcorn is a cheerful nod to that optimistic jackalope and his timeless lessons. As he once advised: "Sometimes you're up, and sometimes you're down." And when you are down, you just have to rebound . . . preferably with a tasty bowl of popcorn.

3 tablespoons vegetable oil

¼ cup popcorn kernels

2 tablespoons salted butter

½ teaspoon dried sage

½ teaspoon Himalayan pink salt

Heat the oil in a large pot over medium heat.

Add a couple kernels of popcorn to the pot and cover, waiting for them to pop. Once they pop, the oil is ready, and you can add the rest of the popcorn.

Place the lid on the pot and wait for the popcorn to pop, shaking the pot slightly every 20 seconds to allow all kernels to get an even distribution of heat.

Once popping slows down (only hearing 1 pop every 10 seconds), remove the pot from the heat and transfer popcorn to a large serving bowl.

Melt the butter in a microwave for 45 seconds, then pour over the top of the popcorn.

Sprinkle the sage and salt on top and then mix, so all popcorn has an even amount of butter, sage, and salt.

FUN FACT

The jackalope from *Boundin'* appears on the back of one of the motor homes in the opening race sequence in *Cars*.

The Incredibles, 2004

FROZONE SLUSHIE

Drink | YIELD: 1 serving | Vegetarian, Vegan, Dairy Free, Gluten Free

As Mr. Incredible's lifelong super-friend, Frozone is quick to jump into action whenever Mr. Incredible calls. And while Frozone must occasionally ask, "Where is my super suit?" his icy powers are always primed and ready—so long as he doesn't get thirsty. The refreshing Frozone Slushie would make an incredible kickoff to a night spent saving the city. Tart lemonade and sweet blueberries come together in a lightly blended slush that's sure to leave anyone feeling properly hydrated. And having seconds is always encouraged—after all, we *are* talking about the greater good!

2 cups ice

1 cup lemonade

1 lemon wedge

1 tablespoon granulated sugar

¼ cup blueberries

SPECIAL TOOLS NEEDED:

Blender

Blend the ice and lemonade in a blender for 30 seconds or until fully mixed and a slushie consistency.

Run the wedge of lemon around the rim of your glass.

Place the sugar on a small plate and roll the rim of your glass into the sugar.

Place the blueberries at the bottom of the glass, then fill with the slushie.

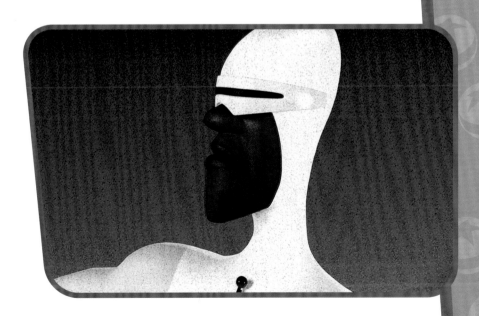

MOVIE SPOTLIGHT:
CARS

Memorable Quote: "Ka-chow!"

Release Years: *Cars* (2006), *Cars 2* (2011), *Cars 3* (2017)

Directors: John Lasseter and Joe Ranft (*Cars*, *Cars 2*), Brian Fee (*Cars 3*)

Lightning McQueen is a race car through and through. For Lightning, "I am speed" is more than just a mantra—it's a way of life. He throws himself into his job, eschewing friends for corporate sponsors and vacations for race days with his trusty hauler, Mack. But when he finds himself stranded in the sleepy town of Radiator Springs, he's suddenly adrift. The one-stoplight town has no proper racetrack, no press junkets, and as far as Lightning's concerned, absolutely no reason to stick around. But Lightning quickly discovers that a change in routine—even one mandated by the court—might be just what he needs to finally become who he's meant to be . . . and to settle down in a town worth fixing.

Released in 2006, *Cars* immediately captured the hearts of families and fans around the world. Its characters were embraced with immense enthusiasm—from confident race car Lightning McQueen to plucky tow truck Tow Mater to the wise (and occasionally grumpy) Doc, the town lawyer Sally, and of course, Snotrod, Wingo, DJ, and Boost—the drifters whose wild antics literally launched Lightning on his path to Radiator Springs. The film was so popular that it inspired two sequels—*Cars 2* (2011), and *Cars 3* (2017). And on June 13, 2012, Pixar debuted the fully immersive Cars Land in Disney's California Adventure. For the first time, fans were able to step inside the world of one of their favorite Pixar films. They walked past Doc Hudson's Piston Cups, touched the beloved statue of Radiator Springs' founder, Stanley, and dined at the famed Flo's V-8 Café—where the on-screen cars had frequently swapped stories over refreshing cans of fuel. And although the connection between cars and food may not be an immediate one—after all, the cars themselves preferred gasoline and oil to Cars Land dishes like the Ka-Cheeseburger and Ramone's Low and Slow Club—there's no denying that Flo's V-8 Café truly speaks to fans' hearts . . . by way of their stomachs! Further down the road at the Cozy Cone Motel—a series of orange traffic cones located across from Flo's V-8 Café—*Cars* aficionados can dine on treats that range from Chili Cone Queso to Fillmore's Fuelin' Groovy All Natural Lemonade. Visitors are seen walking the street carrying bubbly beverages in their very own Cozy Cones—a nod to the hotel where Lightning stayed during his court-imposed sentence . . . and began to fall in love with the little town, and its inspiring attorney/innkeeper, Sally.

Cars reminds us to slow down, appreciate life's moments, and "stop and smell the oil cans"—whether those cans are filled with the more conventional Dinoco, or Fillmore's original, home-brewed organic fuel. And Mater shows us all that memories created alongside friends are among life's greatest joys—from learning the importance of avoiding the pistachio ice cream in *Cars 2* ("It has turned!") to cheering Lightning on as he embarks on a new phase of his career in *Cars 3*. With loyalty, friendship, and found family at its core, it's no wonder that *Cars* has become one of Pixar's most beloved franchises. Ka-chow!

Cars, 2006

LUIGI'S TOWER OF TIRES PASTA SALAD

Side | YIELD: 8 servings | Vegetarian

The little car Luigi is immensely proud of his Italian heritage. He brings a slice of Italy to Radiator Springs with his Leaning Tower of Tires. This twist on a classic Italian dish is inspired by the whitewall tires Luigi proudly displays in his shop. Luigi's Tower of Tires Pasta Salad combines wagon wheel pasta into a delicious salad that will make diners want to scream their excitement to the world . . . just like Luigi!

16 ounces rotelle (wagon wheel) pasta

½ cup grated Parmesan cheese

½ teaspoon garlic powder

¼ teaspoon dried parsley

⅛ teaspoon kosher salt

⅛ teaspoon black pepper

¼ cup olive oil

1 cup cherry tomatoes

1 cup fresh mozzarella pearls

1 cup medium black olives

Cook the pasta al dente in a large pot of water according to directions on the package.

While the pasta cooks, prepare the seasoning mixture. Mix the grated Parmesan, garlic powder, parsley, salt, and pepper in a small bowl. Set aside.

Drain the pasta, rinse with cold water, and place in a large bowl. Mix in the olive oil. Sprinkle the seasoning on top and toss to coat. Mix in the cherry tomatoes, mozzarella pearls, and olives.

Serve chilled or at room temperature.

Cars, 2006

KA-CHOW COFFEE

Drink | YIELD: 1 serving | Vegetarian, Vegan, Dairy Free, Gluten Free

Racing sensation Lightning McQueen knows that he's a precision instrument of speed and aerodynamics. "I am speed" isn't just his mantra—it's his way of life. And it's powered him through countless victories, from that first, hard-won Piston Cup to the altogether exhilarating World Grand Prix. But races aren't won without a solid pit crew . . . and a healthy dose of the best fuel around. Ka-Chow Coffee is a unique blend of percolating power that's designed to boost a racer straight through to the finish line. Coffee, sugar, and espresso come together in an energetic brew that's garnered quite the following—with good reason! Just one sip and race cars and tired fans alike will be gunning for victory. Ka-chow!

½ cup granulated sugar

¼ cup water

2 cups ice

8 ounces drip coffee

1 shot espresso

SPECIAL TOOLS NEEDED:

Shaker

Place the sugar and water in a small pan and heat over medium heat, stirring often, until the sugar and water form a simple syrup. Place in the refrigerator to cool.

Fill a shaker halfway with ice, and then pour in the coffee, espresso, and 1 ounce of simple syrup. Shake until chilled.

Fill a tall glass with ice and strain the drink into the glass. Stir in additional simple syrup to taste.

FUN FACT

Lightning McQueen's name is in honor of Glenn McQueen, a Pixar animator who worked on the film and passed away during its production.

Cars, 2006

HOMEMADE ORGANIC FUEL

Drink | **YIELD:** 1 serving | Vegetarian, Vegan, Dairy Free, Gluten Free

The laid-back hippy van Fillmore knows that it's futile to resist change. He's a firm believer in flower power, auto yoga, and of course, organic everything. Inspired by his lifestyle, this green smoothie would make a fine addition to the menu at Fillmore's Taste-In. Made from spinach, chia seeds, and pineapple, Homemade Organic Fuel is so good that even Sarge would approve. Groovy, man!

1 cup frozen spinach

½ cup frozen pineapple

1 banana

1 green apple, peeled, cored, and diced

¾ cup almond milk

½ tablespoon chia seeds

Place the spinach, pineapple, banana, apple, almond milk, and chia seeds into a blender.

Blend for 1 minute or until smooth.

Pour into a glass.

SPECIAL TOOLS NEEDED:

Blender

FUN FACT

The sounds of the bugs in the movie are actual VW Bug sounds, sped up.

MOVIE SPOTLIGHT:
RATATOUILLE

Memorable Quote: "If you are what you eat, then I only want to eat the good stuff."

Release Year: 2007

Director: Brad Bird

When epi-curious rat Remy dreams of becoming a chef, he knows he faces an uphill battle. Not only does his father loathe everything to do with humans (especially their fondness for fine food!), but Remy happens to be the one creature no chef *ever* wants to find in his kitchen. It doesn't help that Remy has a highly developed sense of taste and smell—a mixed blessing that initially lands him in the undesirable position of being his rat colony's poison sniffer. But after years of determining which discarded food scraps are suitable for his friends and family to eat, he's able to put his gift to use. A surprising intersection with the human world leads Remy to a partnership with the clumsy junior chef Linguini . . . and sets the unusual duo on a path to culinary greatness. Scintillating, inspiring, and a beautiful ode to both the city of Paris and French cuisine, *Ratatouille* brilliantly illustrates the fervent belief of famed food critic Anton Ego: "A great artist can come from anywhere."

Remy's interactions with food are among the film's most touching. When the little rat pairs a hunk of cheese with a solitary strawberry, the tastes combine in an explosion of flavor . . . which Remy imagines as an extravaganza of fireworks. When Anton Ego takes a bite of his beloved childhood ratatouille, he's instantly transported back in time—and immersed in the memory of the meals his mother lovingly prepared to welcome him home after a rough day at school. And when Remy adds ingredients to a bubbling pot, he leaps joyfully along the rim, celebrating the realization of his lifelong dream. The food in *Ratatouille* never just sits in the background. Rather, it is an integral part of the story, moving the plot and allowing viewers a glimpse into the inner lives of the characters—from a persnickety food critic to one ever-hopeful rat.

To depict the world of Parisian cooking in its most realistic light, *Ratatouille's* creative team spent time in the fabled city, observing the architecture and dining at famed restaurants from Le Taillevent to Chez Michel. With food as a main character in this culinary-centered masterpiece, Pixar filmmakers attended cooking classes to better understand the design and functionality of a proper French kitchen. Back home, they furthered their study by working alongside world-famous chef Thomas Keller at his renowned Napa Valley restaurant The French Laundry. And when they sat down at their drawing tables, Pixar artists created 211 different cooking tools to place within Gusteau's kitchen. Their hard work and dedication clearly paid off—*Ratatouille* became an instant classic, garnering a loyal following among Pixar fans. Remy's adventures have since been immortalized in two Disney parks. Disneyland Paris's Walt Disney Studios Park hosts both the ride Ratatouille: The Adventure and the restaurant Bistro Chez Rémy, while Walt Disney World's EPCOT Center is home to the ride Remy's Ratatouille Adventure. Guests queue up to see the world through a rat's point of view . . . and taste the dishes that are so delightfully distinct.

At its heart, *Ratatouille* is quintessentially Pixar—filled with hope, innovation, and of course, a willingness to push through to uncharted territory. After all, not everyone can become a great artist . . . but a great artist can come from anywhere. *Bon appétit!*

Ratatouille, 2007

REMY'S "LIGHTNING-Y" MUSHROOMS

Appetizer | YIELD: 6 mushrooms | Vegetarian, Gluten Free

Every once in a while, culinary lightning strikes. For a certain French gastronome (who also happens to be a rat!), that moment involved a literal bolt of lightning. But Remy's rooftop cooking accident turned out to be just the thing he needed to spark a particularly inspired recipe. Remy's "Lightning-y" Mushrooms invoke all the smoky flavor of the original cheese-and-mushroom dish but with none of the shocking aftertaste. Smooth, savory, and melt-in-your-mouth delicious, these broiled mushrooms will have everyone at the table begging for more, *s'il vous plaît*!

2 tablespoons olive oil

½ tablespoon dried rosemary

½ tablespoon balsamic vinegar

½ teaspoon honey

½ teaspoon freshly ground black pepper

¼ teaspoon kosher salt

3 strands saffron

Pinch of red pepper

6 chanterelle mushrooms (or oyster or cremini mushrooms, if chanterelles aren't available)

4 ounces Tomme de Chèvre cheese (or another aged goat cheese)

Preheat the oven to broil and move a rack to the top spot. Place aluminum foil over a baking sheet and set aside.

In a medium bowl, whisk together the olive oil, rosemary, balsamic vinegar, honey, black pepper, salt, saffron, and red pepper until emulsified. Set aside.

Clean the mushrooms and trim off the ends of the stems. Place the mushrooms in the bowl of marinade and mix so the mushrooms are all fully covered.

Place the mushrooms stem side up on the baking sheet and broil for 3 minutes.

Remove the sheet from the oven, carefully flip the mushrooms right side up, and top each mushroom with a small slice of cheese. Broil for another 2 minutes or until cheese and mushrooms are lightly charred.

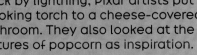

FUN FACT

To figure out what a mushroom would look like after being struck by lightning, Pixar artists put the flame of a cooking torch to a cheese-covered chanterelle mushroom. They also looked at the shapes and textures of popcorn as inspiration.

Ratatouille, 2007

GUSTEAU'S SOUP

Appetizer | YIELD: 8 bowls of soup | Vegetarian, Gluten Free

Sometimes the best recipes come together through a series of happy accidents. Gusteau's famous soup (Remy's version, that is!) never would have existed if Linguini hadn't ruined his own batch. But thanks to some quick thinking—and a highly unusual partnership—a new version of that soup became the hit of Paris . . . and launched Remy onto a path he never could have imagined. With tomatoes, spices, and a solid helping of cream, this interpretation of Gusteau's newest *classique* is sure to please even the toughest of food critics.

2 tablespoons unsalted butter

1 yellow onion, diced

3 cloves garlic, minced

6 large tomatoes, diced

3 cups vegetable stock

One 6-ounce can tomato paste

3 yellow potatoes, cubed

¼ cup fresh basil, chopped

1 tablespoon granulated sugar

1 teaspoon dried thyme

½ teaspoon freshly ground black pepper

⅛ teaspoon cayenne pepper

⅛ teaspoon red pepper flakes

2 bay leaves

2 scallions, thinly sliced

1 leek, sliced thin

1 cup heavy cream

Parsley for garnish

SPECIAL TOOLS NEEDED:

Immersion blender

In a large pot, melt the butter over medium heat. Add the onion and garlic and cook for 3 minutes, or until the onions are translucent and the mixture is fragrant.

Add the tomatoes, vegetable stock, tomato paste, potatoes, basil, sugar, thyme, black pepper, cayenne pepper, and red pepper flakes. Bring to a boil, then reduce heat to medium-low, cover, and let simmer for 20 minutes. Remove the potatoes and place aside in a bowl.

Remove the pot from the heat and purée with an immersion blender or carefully move the soup to a standard blender and purée until smooth.

Return the soup to the pot and onto the heat. Add the potatoes back in, and add the bay leaves, scallions, and leek. Stir in the heavy cream. Simmer for another 10 minutes on medium-low heat.

Serve in a bowl with a sprig of parsley for garnish.

FUN FACT

Linguini's first name is Alfredo.

Ratatouille, 2007

RAT-ATOUILLE

Entrée | YIELD: 8 servings | Vegetarian, Vegan, Dairy Free, Gluten Free

The famed critic Anton Ego once said, "Not everyone can become a great artist; but a great artist can come from anywhere." And this classic French dish is sure to win raves of approval for any who are bold enough to prepare it. Basil, thyme, and oregano season a magnificent medley of vegetables. These ingredients come together to evoke warm memories of childhood games in the garden, families gathering together, and of course, the familiar, all-encompassing warmth that comes from sharing a home-cooked meal. This flavorful Rat-atouille is sure to be an instant classic . . . wherever it happens to be made.

PIPERADE:

1 tablespoon olive oil

1 yellow onion, diced

1 red pepper, diced

1 yellow pepper, diced

10 cloves garlic, minced

One 15-ounce can of tomato sauce

1 teaspoon dried basil

1 teaspoon dried thyme

1 teaspoon dried oregano

¼ teaspoon red pepper flakes

¼ teaspoon kosher salt

¼ teaspoon freshly ground black pepper

TO MAKE THE PIPERADE:

Preheat the oven to 350°F.

Heat the olive oil in a large pan over medium-high heat, and then add the diced onion, red and yellow peppers, and garlic. Sauté for 5 minutes or until onion and peppers are softened. Add the tomato sauce, basil, thyme, oregano, red pepper flakes, salt, and ground pepper and let simmer for 3 to 5 minutes or until slightly reduced.

Remove the pan from the heat and purée with an immersion blender or carefully move the soup to a standard blender and purée until smooth. Set aside ¼ cup and spread the rest on the bottom of a large casserole dish or rimmed baking sheet.

VEGETABLES:

1 zucchini

1 Japanese eggplant (or a baby eggplant, if Japanese is not available)

1 yellow squash

3 Roma tomatoes

1 tablespoon olive oil

½ teaspoon garlic powder

¼ teaspoon thyme

Pinch of salt and pepper

FINISHING SAUCE:

¼ cup piperade

1 tablespoon olive oil

1 teaspoon white balsamic vinegar

Parsley, for garnish

Chives, for garnish

SPECIAL TOOLS NEEDED:

Immersion blender

Mandoline

TO MAKE THE VEGETABLES:

Using a mandoline, slice the zucchini, eggplant, yellow squash, and tomatoes into thin, even slices. Stack them and fan them out around the casserole dish, alternating vegetables.

Mix the olive oil, garlic powder, thyme, salt, and pepper in a small bowl. Drizzle over the top of the vegetables.

Place parchment paper over the top of the vegetables and bake for 30 minutes. Remove the parchment paper and bake for another 30 minutes.

Take a small portion out and place delicately in the middle of a plate. Mix the piperade you set aside with the olive oil and vinegar. Drizzle the vinaigrette around the ratatouille stack, and sprinkle parsley leaves around the plate. Cut 1-inch lengths of chives and place one on top of each stack. Serve to the harshest critic you know.

FUN FACT

Chef Thomas Keller of the world-famous French Laundry restaurant in Napa Valley created the ratatouille served to Anton Ego at the end of the film.

Ratatouille, 2007

MAGNIFIQUE LAYER CAKE

Dessert | YIELD: 1 cake | Vegetarian

Cake is a guaranteed crowd-pleaser. And while chocolate, seven layer, and carrot cakes each have their ardent fans, this Magnifique Layer Cake is sure to be the talk of the town— just like a certain rat's five-star, off-the-menu feasts! Sugar, vanilla bean, and a small twist of lemon blend in a tantalizing medley alongside custard, chocolate sauce, and a dab of strawberry whipped cream. It's the perfect combination of zesty sweetness that's sure to earn rave reviews from foodies of all species. After all, if you are what you eat, it's important to eat the good stuff!

CRÈME PÂTISSIÈRE:

2 cups milk

⅓ cup granulated sugar

Pinch of salt

2½ tablespoons cornstarch

1 tablespoon vanilla

3 egg yolks

1 egg

3 tablespoons unsalted butter

CAKE:

1 cup all-purpose flour, plus more for dusting

6 eggs, at room temperature

⅓ cup granulated sugar

¼ teaspoon salt

2 teaspoons vanilla

1 teaspoon lemon zest

3 tablespoons cornstarch

TO MAKE THE CRÈME PÂTISSIÈRE:

Heat the milk over medium heat in a small saucepan until it starts to boil, then remove from heat. Mix the sugar, salt, cornstarch, vanilla, egg yolks, and egg in a small bowl and whisk together. Slowly pour half of the hot milk into the egg mixture while whisking constantly. Once fully mixed, add the mixture into the saucepan with the rest of the milk. Heat the custard over medium heat for 1 to 2 minutes while whisking constantly, lowering the heat if it starts to boil. Remove from the heat and whisk in the butter. Place custard in a bowl and cover with plastic wrap, allowing the wrap to touch the surface of the custard. Refrigerate for a couple hours until it's fully chilled.

TO MAKE THE CAKE:

Preheat the oven to 325°F. Grease and flour the bottom of three 8-inch round cake pans.

Place the eggs, sugar, salt, vanilla, and lemon zest in the bowl of a stand mixer and mix on high for about 5 minutes, until the mixture is light and fluffy.

Mix the flour and cornstarch in a small bowl, and fold into the egg mixture.

Pour a third of the batter into each cake pan and bake for 10 to 12 minutes, or until the cake springs back when gently pressed and a toothpick comes out clean.

Let cool for 5 minutes in the pan, then place on a cooling rack to cool fully.

TOPPING:

½ cup freeze-dried strawberries

1 cup whipping cream

3 tablespoons powdered sugar

½ teaspoon vanilla

Pinch of kosher salt

¼ cup simple syrup

Chocolate sauce, to drizzle

SPECIAL TOOLS NEEDED:

Three 8-inch cake pans

Food processor

TO MAKE THE TOPPING:

While cooling, make the whipped cream topping. Pulse the freeze-dried strawberries in a food processor until they're a fine powder. Place ¼ cup of the strawberry dust, the whipping cream, powdered sugar, vanilla, and salt in a stand mixer fitted with a whisk. Whisk until the mixture forms whipped cream, about 1 to 2 minutes.

Place one layer of cake on a large plate. Brush with half of the simple syrup, then top with half of the custard. Place another layer on top, then brush with the rest of the simple syrup and top with the rest of the custard. Top with the final layer and spread the whipped cream over the top. Drizzle with chocolate sauce.

FUN FACT

The character Bomb Voyage from *The Incredibles* makes two appearances in *Ratatouille*. He appears as a mime on the bridge by Notre Dame when Linguini and Colette skate past. You will have to look very closely to find his second appearance.

Ratatouille, 2007

REMY'S FLIGHT OF FLAVOR

Appetizer | YIELD: 1 board, approximately 12 servings | Vegetarian

Finding good ingredients doesn't have to be a complicated endeavor. It can be as simple as heading to the garden, stopping by the store, or in the case of some particularly resourceful rodents, sneaking tastes from a Parisian country home and savoring the delightful discovery of each delicious flavor combination. And while Remy challenged his fellow rodents to source ingredients from locations *other* than the back alley, he also showed them that a great meal can come from anywhere—so long as it's prepared with love. However a chef procures their food, the key to crafting fine cuisine boils down to creating with confidence. And in the case of this particular tasting board, there's no cooking required! Cheeses, fruits, crackers, and more are placed in an artfully arranged display to create a Flight of Flavor that's fit for a king . . . or a rat! Try each item individually or together to create new flavor sensations, just like Remy did when he combined strawberries and cheese!

1 large green apple

1 pint strawberries

Large bunch red grapes

2 sprigs rosemary

5 basil leaves

One 4-ounce wedge of Brie

One 4-ounce wedge of Gouda

¼ cup honey

¼ cup Marcona almonds

12 savory crackers

12 butter cookies

SPECIAL TOOLS NEEDED:

Large wood board

Cheese knives

Rinse the apple, strawberries, grapes, rosemary, and basil and let dry on a paper towel–lined plate.

Place the wedges of cheese on opposite sides of the board and pair with small cheese knives.

Pour some honey into a small bowl and place on the board with a small spoon. Place Marcona almonds in another small bowl.

Place the grapes on the board.

Slice the green apple and fan across the board.

Fan out the savory crackers on one side of the board and the butter cookies on the other.

Scatter the strawberries throughout the board, filling in any empty spots.

Garnish with rosemary and basil.

Savor each ingredient alone and mixed with each other. Drizzle honey over cheese, take a bite of a strawberry and a basil leaf together, get creative!

FUN FACT

To create a realistic-looking compost pile, Pixar artists photographed and researched the way real produce rots. Fifteen different kinds of produce were left to rot and then photographed, such as apples, berries, bananas, mushrooms, oranges, broccoli, and lettuce.

Ratatouille, 2007

ANYONE CAN COOK SOUFFLÉ

Dessert | YIELD: 4 soufflés | Vegetarian

Renowned chef Auguste Gusteau inspired the world—and one particularly plucky rodent—by insisting that anyone can cook. He believed that limits should never be defined by one's place of origin. This particular stroke of wisdom should truly be taken to heart. Anyone Can Cook Soufflé is a nod to the ever-encouraging chef, whose kind words and inspirational spirit helped show the world that true greatness can come from anyone—so long as they believe in themselves.

1 tablespoon unsalted butter, for greasing soufflé dishes

1 cup granulated sugar, plus more for coating soufflé dishes

½ cup milk

1½ cups crème fraîche

4 egg yolks

⅓ cup all-purpose flour

1 teaspoon cornstarch

2 teaspoons vanilla

2 egg whites

Dash of kosher salt

¼ cup powdered sugar

SPECIAL TOOLS NEEDED:

Four 8-ounce soufflé dishes or ramekins

Preheat the oven to 375°F. Butter four 8-ounce ramekins or soufflé dishes and then dust the buttered insides with granulated sugar. (This will prevent the soufflés from sticking.) Set the ramekins on a rimmed baking sheet or casserole dish and set aside.

In a large pot, heat the milk and crème fraîche over medium-low for 2 minutes or until steaming but not boiling.

Mix the egg yolks and sugar together in a medium bowl until fully mixed and pale. Whisk in the flour and cornstarch until a thick batter consistency.

Pour ⅓ of the hot milk mixture into the batter and stir quickly to temper the yolks, not allowing them to cook. Pour this batter mixture back into the pot with the rest of the milk and turn the heat to medium-high. Bring to a boil and cook for 1 to 2 minutes, stirring constantly, until thickened.

Remove from heat and stir in the vanilla. Set aside.

Place the egg whites and a dash of salt in the bowl of a stand mixer with a whisk attachment and whisk until stiff peaks form (about 4 minutes).

Gradually fold the whipped egg whites into the batter, and then divide the mixture evenly between the four ramekins.

Bake for 25 to 30 minutes or until golden and puffed. Do not open the oven door while they're baking, or the risen tops of the soufflés may fall!

Dust with powdered sugar and serve immediately.

FUN FACT

When he was alive, Gusteau was 6 feet 10 inches tall.

Presto, 2008

PRESTO CARROTS

Side | YIELD: 2 servings | Vegetarian, Gluten Free

For proud magician Presto DiGiotagione, magic isn't quite as simple as pulling a rabbit out of a hat—especially when the rabbit in question has a mind of its own! Luckily for Presto, even rabbits have their weaknesses. And these Presto Carrots are bound to be a mighty motivator for even the most recalcitrant assistant. Sweetened with honey and cooked to perfection, Presto Carrots will disappear as fast as you can say, "Alec Azam!"

1 pound young carrots with the tops still on, washed, scrubbed, and dried

2 tablespoons unsalted butter, melted

2 tablespoons honey

1 teaspoon dried thyme

Dash of kosher salt

Dash of freshly ground black pepper

Preheat the oven to 400°F. Line a baking sheet with foil and place the carrots on the sheet.

In a small bowl, mix the butter, honey, thyme, salt, and pepper. Pour the mixture over the carrots and toss to coat.

Bake the carrots for 30 minutes, turning halfway through, until tender and browned.

Remove from the oven and make them disappear!

WALL•E, 2008

NEVER-EXPIRED CAKE

Dessert | YIELD: 16 cakes | Vegetarian

It's not easy being one of the last beings on Earth. Supplies are finite, and companions are few and far between. But one unlikely discovery can turn a monotonous existence into a cause for celebration. Inspired by *WALL•E*, this Never-Expired Cake pairs a sweetened dough with a thick, creamy filling. It's a deceptively simple dessert that evokes feelings of nostalgia—an emotion WALL•E experiences while watching one of his favorite human films, *Hello Dolly*. There's lots of world out there, just waiting to be explored. And this cake is perfect to share with the one you want to explore it all with.

CAKE:

2 cups cake flour

1 cup granulated sugar, divided

2 teaspoons baking powder

1 teaspoon kosher salt

6 eggs

¼ teaspoon cream of tartar

½ cup whole milk

⅔ cup canola oil

1 tablespoon vanilla

FILLING:

4 tablespoons unsalted butter, softened

⅓ cup marshmallow fluff

1 tablespoon heavy cream

½ teaspoon vanilla

Pinch of kosher salt

1 cup powdered sugar

SPECIAL TOOLS NEEDED:

Eclair molds

Chopstick

TO MAKE THE CAKES:

Preheat the oven to 350°F. Grease the eclair molds and set aside.

Combine the flour, ¾ cup sugar, baking powder, and salt in a medium bowl. Set aside.

Separate the eggs and place the whites in the bowl of a stand mixer with a whisk attachment. Beat the egg whites until foamy, about 30 seconds. Add the remaining ¼ cup sugar and the cream of tartar to the egg whites, and beat until soft peaks form, 4 to 5 minutes.

In a large bowl, whisk together the egg yolks, milk, oil, and vanilla. Fold in the egg white mixture.

Pour the dry ingredients into the wet ingredients slowly, mixing while pouring. Whisk until smooth.

Fill the eclair molds ⅔ full.

Bake for 13 to 15 minutes or until the cakes spring back to the touch.

TO MAKE THE FILLING:

Mix the butter, marshmallow fluff, cream, vanilla, and salt in the bowl of a stand mixer until light and fluffy, about 2 minutes. Add in the powdered sugar slowly on low speed. Mix for another minute on medium speed. Place the filling in a piping bag or zippered plastic bag and set aside.

Once the cake is finished baking, let cool on a wire rack. Once cooled, poke three holes in the center of one of the edges of the cake with the chopstick. Poke lengthwise throughout the cake, but don't go all the way through.

Cut the edge of the piping/zippered bag and fill the three holes with the filling. Repeat for each cake.

FUN FACT

The following items/characters from past Pixar films can be found in WALL·E's trailer and the trash on Earth: Rex the dinosaur, a Buzz Lightyear lunchbox from *Toy Story*, a Lightning McQueen toy from *Cars*, the snow globe from the short film *Knick Knack*, the bug zapper from *A Bug's Life*, and an antenna ball of Mike Wazowski from *Monsters, Inc.*

AXIOM CUPCAKE IN A CUP

Dessert | YIELD: 1 milkshake | Vegetarian

There's no finer way to celebrate the 700-year anniversary of a luxury space cruiser than with an Axiom Cupcake in a Cup. This creamy, vanilla milkshake blends ice cream and milk with a festive cupcake, whipping them together in a frothy concoction that's quickly become the talk of the Axiom. Topped with whipped cream, sprinkles, and strawberry sauce, this otherworldly treat is the ultimate way to mark a septicentennial in space. . . or a celebratory occasion right here on Earth!

2 cups vanilla ice cream

½ cup whole milk

1 vanilla cupcake

Simple syrup, for rimming the glass

Nonpareil sprinkles, for rimming the glass

Whipped cream, for topping

Strawberry sauce, for topping

Sprinkles, for topping

SPECIAL TOOLS NEEDED:

Blender

Place the ice cream, milk, and cupcake in a blender. Blend for 30 seconds or until fully mixed.

Place the simple syrup on a plate and the nonpareil sprinkles on a separate plate. Dip an upside-down glass into the simple syrup, so the top rim is coated in the simple syrup. Dip the syrup-coated rim into the plate of nonpareil sprinkles, coating it.

Pour the milkshake into the glass and top with whipped cream, drizzles of strawberry sauce, and a shake of sprinkles.

FUN FACT

The infamous Pizza Planet truck is one of the items EVE scans on Earth.

Partly Cloudy, 2009

THE CLOUDY CONCOCTION

Drink | YIELD: 1 serving | Vegetarian, Vegan, Dairy Free, Gluten Free

To anyone who's ever thought their job was stressful, the baby-delivering storks and their cloudy counterparts would like to point out that no human—no matter how occupationally frazzled—has *ever* had to deliver a quill-shooting porcupette or a sharp-toothed shark pup. But, employee loyalty is always rewarded—in the human workplace, as well as in the baby-delivery business. And The Cloudy Concoction is a dream-worthy drink, perfect for sharing with a tired colleague or tried-and-true friend. With two layers of cotton candy and a hearty spritz of ginger ale, this beverage is sure to lighten any mood, no matter what life—*or work!*—tosses out next!

1 cup blue cotton candy, plus more for garnish

6 ounces ginger ale

1 ounce lemon juice

Ice

Place the cotton candy at the bottom of a glass and pour the ginger ale and lemon juice on top, melting the candy.

Mix the beverage and top with ice and a "cloud" of cotton candy.

FUN FACT

At the beginning of *Partly Cloudy*, Ellie from *Up* can be seen accepting a baby in the window.

Up, 2009

SPIRIT OF ADVENTURE SPECIAL

Entrée | YIELD: 2 servings | Gluten Free

Charles Muntz's well-known ship inspired a generation of explorers. And although it's been said one should never meet their heroes, it is highly advisable to taste a hero's signature dish—especially when that dish is a decidedly decadent treat! The Spirit of Adventure Special pairs seared scallops with caviar in a delightfully lavish feast that's sure to inspire anyone to seek out adventure—no zeppelin required.

2 leeks

½ teaspoon kosher salt, divided

½ teaspoon freshly ground black pepper, divided

3 tablespoons olive oil, divided

6 scallops

2 tablespoons salted butter

1 tablespoon caviar

2 sprigs parsley, for garnish

Prepare the leeks by cutting the ends and green leaves off, leaving only the white/light green stalk. Cut in half lengthwise and wash well, rinsing between all of the layers.

Discard the thick outer layers of the leek and rest the leek on a paper towel to dry. Season with ¼ teaspoon of both salt and pepper.

Heat 2 tablespoons of olive oil in a large skillet over medium heat, then add the leeks.

Cook for 6 to 8 minutes, turning halfway through, until tender and lightly browned. Set aside.

Pat the scallops dry with a paper towel and season with the remaining ¼ teaspoons salt and pepper.

Place the other tablespoon olive oil in the skillet and turn the heat to medium-high.

Once oil is hot, add the scallops and let cook in place for 2 minutes or until the bottom is seared. Turn over and cook for another 2 minutes, until both sides are seared a golden brown. While waiting for the final side to cook, add the butter to the pan, allowing it to melt around the scallops.

Place two leek halves on each of two plates, followed by three scallops. Balance ½ tablespoon caviar on one scallop from each plate and add a parsley garnish.

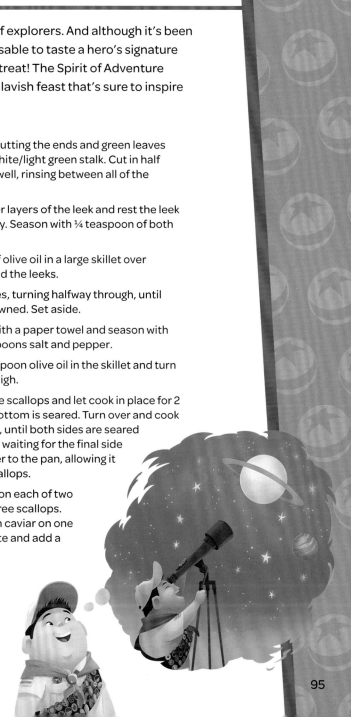

FUN FACT

Muntz's jacket is the first time in Pixar history where they had to make a cloth garment out of fur. No CG animals were harmed.

BALLOON BOUQUET CAKE POPS

Dessert | YIELD: 50 cake pops | Vegetarian

Carl has always dreamed of adventure. And with a little work—and a *lot* of ingenuity—his dreams might just take flight. Inspired by Carl's remarkable experience, these Balloon Bouquet Cake Pops offer an instant pick-me-up. Loaded with chocolate and coated in bright candy colors, these mini-balloons serve as a tasty reminder of one of life's greatest truths: Adventure is out there!

CAKE:

4 tablespoons instant coffee powder

1½ cups milk

2 cups all-purpose flour

2 cups granulated sugar

1 cup unsweetened cocoa powder

1 teaspoon baking soda

1 teaspoon baking powder

½ teaspoon kosher salt

⅔ cup canola oil

2 teaspoons vanilla

2 eggs

FROSTING:

1½ cups unsalted butter

3 cups powdered sugar

½ cup cocoa powder

1 teaspoon vanilla

Dash of kosher salt

DECORATION:

24 ounces assorted colored candy melts

TO MAKE THE CAKE:

Preheat the oven to 350°F and oil a 13-by-9-inch cake pan/casserole dish. Set aside.

In a small bowl, mix the instant coffee powder into the milk. Set aside.

In a large mixing bowl, sift together the flour, sugar, cocoa powder, baking soda, baking powder, and salt. Add the milk mixture, oil, and vanilla.

Mix on low speed until combined, then mix on medium speed for 2 minutes. Add the eggs one at a time and mix for 2 minutes more.

Pour the batter into the cake pan and bake for 25 to 30 minutes or until a toothpick inserted comes out clean. Let cool in the pan for 5 minutes and then move to a rack to cool fully.

TO MAKE THE FROSTING:

Beat the unsalted butter in the bowl of a stand mixer until light and fluffy, about 2 minutes. Slowly add the powdered sugar, ½ cup at a time, mixing fully each time. Add the cocoa powder and mix. Finally, add the vanilla and salt and mix for 2 minutes, or until everything is light, fluffy, and the texture of a thick buttercream frosting.

SPECIAL TOOLS NEEDED:

Cake pop/lollipop sticks

Cake pop stand or foam block

TO ASSEMBLE:

Once cooled, crumble the cake into a fine, sand-like texture in a food processor or large bowl. Add the frosting and mix until a consistent, dough-like texture forms.

Place parchment paper down on a large plate or baking sheet.

Take 1 tablespoon of the cake mixture and form into a ball. Slightly elongate the ball into an oval balloon shape. Place on the baking sheet. Continue with the rest of the mixture.

Freeze for 15 minutes or until chilled and solid.

Melt the candy melts according to package instructions, keeping each color separate and placing each in a deep bowl or glass. Dip the end of a lollipop stick into the melted candy melts and poke into the center bottom of the cake squares, inserting it about halfway. Continue with the rest of the cake pops, then freeze for another 5 minutes. If necessary, re-melt the candy melts to a thin and smooth consistency. Dip one cake pop at a time into the melts, fully coating the cake pop up to the stick. Remove and let any excess come off. Place the cake pop sticks into a cake pop stand or a foam block until set, about 30 minutes.

Combine the multicolored balloons together to form multiple colorful and delicious bouquets of balloons!

FUN FACT

There are 10,297 balloons lifting Carl's house.

Up, 2009

ADVENTURE'S END SUNDAE

Dessert | YIELD: 1 large ice cream sundae (feeds 2 to 4) | Vegetarian, Gluten Free

Every great adventure deserves to be celebrated—preferably with ice cream! Adventure's End Sundae blends Russell's favorite chocolate ice cream with Carl's beloved butter brickle, then tops the concoction off with a thick, butterscotch syrup and a dollop of whipped cream. It's perfect to share with a fellow Wilderness Explorer, a grumpy neighbor-turned-friend, or a talking dog who has just met you but already loves you.

½ cup light brown sugar

¼ cup unsalted butter

½ teaspoon vanilla

Dash of kosher salt

1 pint chocolate ice cream

2 tablespoons butterscotch syrup

¼ cup whipped cream

SPECIAL TOOLS NEEDED:

Candy thermometer

First, make the butter brickle: Mix the brown sugar, butter, vanilla, and salt in a small saucepan over medium heat, and bring to a boil. Cook, stirring often, until a candy thermometer reaches 300°F and the mixture has browned, about 5 minutes.

Pour the hot mixture onto a rimmed baking sheet lined with parchment paper or a silicone baking mat.

Let cool for 20 minutes or until hardened, then break the brickle up into small pieces.

While the brickle is cooling, take the chocolate ice cream out of the freezer and allow it to soften. Once softened, place the ice cream into a large bowl, and mix ¼ cup brickle pieces into the ice cream. Place back into the freezer to refreeze.

When frozen, use an ice cream scoop to scoop out 3 scoops into a large bowl. Drizzle with butterscotch syrup, top with whipped cream, and sprinkle the rest of the butter brickle on top.

Enjoy with your family!

FUN FACT

The Fenton's ice cream parlor in the movie is based on the real Fenton's restaurant in Oakland, California.

Up, 2009

ELLIE'S ADVENTURE

Drink | Yield: 1 large float | Vegetarian, Gluten Free

Childhood sweethearts Carl and Ellie shared a special bond—one forged in friendship and solidified by a homemade grape soda cap pin. Ellie's Adventure pays tribute to this special relationship in a particularly sweet way. Balloon-colored sherbet and a generous pour of grape soda combine in a burst of vibrant color that encapsulates joy, optimism, and of course, love.

4 flavors of sherbet in assorted colors

12 ounces grape soda

SPECIAL TOOLS NEEDED:

Ice cream scoop

Scoop 1 rounded scoop of each sherbet flavor, and place on a parchment paper–lined plate or baking sheet. Freeze for 5 minutes.

Place the frozen scoops into a large glass, and fill with grape soda.

Add two straws and enjoy with your favorite adventure buddy!

FUN FACT

The flight number on Carl and Ellie's Venezuela tickets is 2319—the same as the alert number in *Monsters, Inc.* when George Sanderson has a kid's sock on his back.

CHAPTER THREE
ADVANCES IN TECHNOLOGY

★

2010-2019

Day & Night, 2010

SUNRISE/SUNSET

Drink | YIELD: 2 servings | Vegetarian, Vegan, Dairy Free, Gluten Free

Day and Night have completely different worldviews. After all, a verdant meadow or the glittering lights of Las Vegas are hardly the same in broad daylight as they are under the stars. But for one blissful moment, these two worlds collide in a mirrored moment that's perfectly encapsulated by Sunrise/Sunset. This sparkling beverage incorporates sunny orange juice with midnight-blue dried butterfly pea flowers. Easily transformable with an orange garnish—or an additional pea-flower swirl—Sunrise/Sunset will have even the most confrontational party guests instantly seeing eye to eye.

1 tablespoon dried butterfly pea flowers

1 cup hot water

Ice cubes

8 ounces orange juice

4 ounces lime sparkling water

2 ounces grenadine

½ orange, for garnish

Mix the butterfly pea flowers into a mug filled with the hot water and let steep for 5 minutes, or until dark blue. Strain into a large glass of ice and set aside to cool.

Fill two tall glasses with ice.

Pour 4 ounces orange juice into each glass, and then top off with 2 ounces sparkling water.

Pour 1 ounce grenadine in each glass, allowing it to sink to the bottom.

Cut two round slices from an orange and cut a slit halfway into each round. Place on the top of the glasses as a "sunshine" garnish.

Enjoy as is or transform the drink into a sunset by doing the following: Pour the dark-blue "night" iced tea onto the top of each sunset drink, and give a light mix. Watch it transform colors as it turns the sunrise into a sunset.

Toy Story 3, 2010

JELLY BEAN BURGERS

Dessert | YIELD: 24 burgers | Vegetarian

Some combinations just make sense—like ketchup and mustard, ice cream and sprinkles, and Woody and Buzz. And for Bonnie, no burger is complete without her all-important secret ingredient—jelly beans! This cheerful nod to Bonnie's kid-approved concoction offers chocolate "meat" centers, coconutty "lettuce" toppings, and of course, a smattering of jelly beans. Serve at your next family gathering—or on a playdate with destiny!

YELLOW CAKE:

2½ cups all-purpose flour, plus more for cupcake pans

2½ teaspoons baking powder

½ teaspoon kosher salt

¾ cup unsalted butter, room temperature

1½ cups sugar

3 eggs, room temperature

1½ teaspoons vanilla

1¼ cups whole milk

2 tablespoons cocoa powder

BUTTERCREAM FROSTING:

2 sticks unsalted butter

2 cups powdered sugar

1½ teaspoons vanilla extract

⅛ teaspoon kosher salt

Red, yellow, and green gel food coloring

1 cup shredded coconut

½ cup jelly beans

¼ cup sesame seeds

TO MAKE THE CUPCAKES:

Preheat the oven to 350°F and grease and flour two cupcake pans (for a total of 24 cavities).

Mix the flour, baking powder, and salt in a medium bowl. Set aside.

Beat the butter and sugar together in the bowl of a stand mixer until light and fluffy, about 2 minutes.

Add eggs to the butter mixture, mixing fully between each egg. Mix in the vanilla.

Mix half of the flour mixture into the butter mixture. Add half of the milk and mix. Continue with the rest of the flour mixture and milk. Make sure everything is fully mixed.

Pour half of the cake batter into half of the cupcake cavities, filling each one ⅔ full.

Add the cocoa powder to the remaining cake batter, mix thoroughly, and then fill the remaining empty cupcake cavities with the chocolate batter mixture.

Bake for 20 to 25 minutes, or until a toothpick inserted in the middle comes out clean.

Let cupcakes cool in the pan for about 5 minutes, then carefully transfer to a rack to completely cool.

TO MAKE THE BUTTERCREAM FROSTING:

Put the unsalted butter into the bowl of a stand mixer and mix on medium-high until butter is completely smooth and against the bowl.

Slowly add the powdered sugar to the butter until it is fully mixed.

Add in the vanilla extract and salt and mix until you have a whipped buttercream frosting texture.

Split the buttercream frosting into three separate bowls. Add red coloring to one until it looks like ketchup, add yellow coloring to one until it looks like mustard, and keep one white.

Mix the shredded coconut and a small amount of the green food coloring in a bowl until it looks like shredded lettuce.

TO ASSEMBLE

Slice the yellow cupcakes in half horizontally.

Slice the chocolate cupcakes in thirds horizontally. (You should be able to cut the bottom in half, and then slice a small portion of the rounded bit off the top to create three "meat patties.")

Spread a small amount of the white frosting in the center of the bottom half of the yellow cupcake. Place a brown cupcake "patty" on top.

Place the red and green frostings in separate piping bags or plastic zippered bags, fitted with a small round piping tip. Pipe the frosting around the edges of the brown cupcake "patty." Allowing the frosting to fall over onto the sides will help it show up even more once it's all pieced together!

Place a few jelly beans on top of the frosting, and then sprinkle the coconut "lettuce" over top.

Place the top of the yellow cupcake on top of your mini cupcake burger.

Lightly brush the top of the cupcake with water and sprinkle sesame seeds on top.

FUN FACT

The drawings of Bonnie's toys that are taped to the walls of her bedroom in the epilogue were drawn by director Lee Unkrich's children, Hannah, Alice, and Max.

Cars 2, 2011

LEMON COOKIES

Dessert | YIELD: 24 cookies | Vegetarian, Dairy Free

The Lemons are an international crime syndicate made up of underperforming cars. Their group is determined to get revenge on a world that rejected them for the manufacturing defects that are clearly beyond their control. But while Miles Axlerod, along with help from Acer and Grem, devises his dastardly plot, the Radiator Springs crew proves that friendship can overcome any obstacle. Inspired by the Italian leg of the World Grand Prix, these Lemon Cookies combine olive oil, vanilla, and of course, those persnickety lemons. They're sweet, tangy, and like Lightning McQueen himself, they're sure to give folks a little sizzle.

1¼ cups granulated sugar, divided

⅔ cup olive oil

1 lemon, juiced and zested

1 teaspoon vanilla

1 large egg

2½ cups all-purpose flour

1 teaspoon baking powder

½ teaspoon baking soda

½ teaspoon kosher salt

SPECIAL TOOLS NEEDED:

Small cookie scoop

Preheat the oven to 350°F and line a large baking sheet with parchment paper.

Mix 1 cup sugar, the olive oil, lemon juice, lemon zest, and vanilla in a medium bowl. Add the egg and mix until fully incorporated.

Mix the flour, baking powder, baking soda, and salt in a separate medium bowl. Slowly add it into the sugar mixture, mixing until fully combined.

Place the remaining ¼ cup granulated sugar on a small plate. Use a small cookie scoop (about 1½ tablespoons) to create cookie balls, then roll them in the sugar. Place the sugared cookie dough onto the baking sheet, leaving 1 inch between each cookie.

Bake for 12 to 15 minutes or until the edges are just starting to brown.

Let cool for 5 minutes, then transfer to a wire rack to finish cooling.

FUN FACT

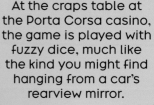

At the craps table at the Porta Corsa casino, the game is played with fuzzy dice, much like the kind you might find hanging from a car's rearview mirror.

La Luna, 2011

LA LUNA PIES

Appetizer | YIELD: 8 pies | Vegetarian

Traditions are important . . . but it's equally important for future generations to forge their own paths. For the young star-sweeper Bambino, that means respecting the old ways embraced by his family, while choosing to do things on his own, unique terms. Inspired by *La Luna*, these cheese pies are a heartwarming tribute to anyone who's ever reached for the stars—or been tasked with cleaning up after them. Cheerful, cheesy, and bursting with flavor, *La Luna* Pies are a savory snack that's meant to be enjoyed by dreamers of all ages.

2 eggs, divided

¾ cup feta cheese, crumbled

½ cup ricotta cheese

¼ cup grated Parmesan cheese

¼ cup shredded Gouda cheese

2 teaspoons fresh dill, minced

½ teaspoon kosher salt

¼ teaspoon freshly ground black pepper

All-purpose flour, for dusting the surface

2 sheets pie crust, thawed

SPECIAL TOOLS NEEDED:

4-inch star-shaped cookie cutter

Preheat the oven to 400°F. Line a baking sheet with parchment paper.

Beat 1 egg in a large bowl, then add the feta, ricotta, Parmesan, and Gouda cheeses, fresh dill, salt, and pepper. Mix.

On a floured surface, roll each pie crust out to a 12-inch square and use a star cookie cutter to cut out 16 equal-sized stars.

Spoon 1 tablespoon of cheese mixture into the center of half of the stars, leaving a ¼-inch border empty around the edges.

Place the unused stars directly on top of the filled stars.

Using a fork, crimp along the edges until each star is fully sealed. Cut a slit into the center top of each pie. Chill the pies in the refrigerator for 15 minutes.

Place the pies on the prepared baking sheet. Beat the remaining egg and brush the tops of the pies with it.

Bake for 20 to 25 minutes or until puffed up and golden brown.

Brave, 2012

WITCH'S CAKES

Dessert | YIELD: 4 tarts | Vegetarian

Witches have a complicated history. They've been known to trick, deceive, and occasionally lash out at those who seek their assistance. But their unorthodox techniques have helped countless spell-seekers to better their lives, deepen their bonds, and even change their fates. This recipe, inspired by the tart that was given to Merida by a certain bear-carving witch, piles cheesecake and cherry filling into a shortbread shell. Sweet, creamy, and delightfully unexpected, these portable pastries conjure the perfect touch of whimsy to brighten any dank chamber . . . or emotionally charged, multi-clan gathering!

CRUST:

1 cup all-purpose flour

⅓ cup powdered sugar

⅛ teaspoon kosher salt

½ cup unsalted butter, cold and diced

CHEESECAKE:

8 ounces cream cheese, at room temperature

½ cup granulated sugar

½ tablespoon cornstarch

¼ teaspoon vanilla extract

¼ teaspoon lemon zest

½ teaspoon lemon juice

Pinch of kosher salt

1 egg, at room temperature

2 tablespoons sour cream, at room temperature

½ cup cherry pie filling

¼ cup powdered sugar, for garnish

SPECIAL TOOLS NEEDED:

Four 4-inch tart pans

Food processor

TO MAKE THE CRUST:

Preheat the oven to 350°F and grease the bottom and sides of the tart pans. Set aside.

Pulse the flour, powdered sugar, and salt in a food processor until mixed. Add the diced butter and pulse until a dough forms.

Roll the dough out to ¼ inch thick and divide into 4 equal parts. Press the dough onto the bottom and sides of the tart pans. Poke the bottom of the dough with a fork multiple times to prevent it from puffing up while baking.

Bake the crusts for 10 minutes, or until golden brown and set. Let cool.

TO MAKE THE CHEESECAKE:

Place the cream cheese in the bowl of a stand mixer and mix on medium until smooth. Reduce the speed to low and slowly add the sugar and cornstarch. Mix for 2 minutes or until light and fluffy. Using a spatula, scrape down the sides of the bowl. Add the vanilla, lemon zest, lemon juice, and salt, and mix for another minute.

Add the egg, mixing fully. Scrape down the sides of the bowl, then add the sour cream. Mix until combined.

Fill each tart crust ¾ full. Bake for 20 to 25 minutes or until centers are almost set. Remove and let cool fully.

Cut out a 1-inch circle in the middle of each tart (leaving the crust intact), and fill with cherry pie filling. Garnish with powdered sugar around the cheesecake portion.

FUN FACT

Merida has more than 1,500 individually sculpted, curly red strands that generate about 111,700 total hairs. If Merida's curls were straightened, her hair would be *four feet* long and reach the middle of her calf.

Brave, 2012

KING'S FEAST TURKEY LEGS

Entrée | YIELD: 4 turkey legs | Dairy Free, Gluten Free

Changing one's fate can be an exhausting feat: There are bears to battle (then protect!), curses to thwart, and old rifts to mend. Luckily, all of that can be managed . . . with the right sustenance, of course! King Fergus's beloved feast food—the ever-popular turkey leg—also happens to make a succulent snack for a modern-day picnic. And because every second counts when preparing to shoot for one's own hand, King's Feast Turkey Legs offer a protein-packed meal that's easy to take on the go. Just don't forget to bring the napkins—preferably styled in Clan DunBroch tartan!

¼ cup granulated sugar

2 tablespoons kosher salt

2 teaspoons garlic powder

1 teaspoon chili powder

1 teaspoon paprika

1 teaspoon freshly ground black pepper

½ teaspoon thyme

½ teaspoon cumin

4 cups water

½ teaspoon liquid smoke

4 turkey legs

¼ cup olive oil

SPECIAL TOOLS NEEDED:

Meat thermometer

In a large bowl or watertight zippered bag, mix the sugar, salt, garlic powder, chili powder, paprika, black pepper, thyme, and cumin. Add the water and liquid smoke and mix to make a brine.

Place the turkey legs in the brine, cover, and let refrigerate overnight (or at least 8 hours).

Preheat the oven to 450°F and line a roasting pan (or a metal rack on top of a casserole dish or baking sheet) with aluminum foil.

Remove the turkey legs from the brine, pat with a paper towel, and rub the legs with olive oil. Place on the roasting pan and cover loosely with aluminum foil.

Bake the legs for 20 to 25 minutes per pound, turning over halfway through. The legs should brown and reach an internal temperature of at least 165°F.

Set the oven to broil and cook the legs for an additional 5 minutes for extra crispy skin.

Let cool for 5 minutes and enjoy!

FUN FACT

In Scotland, there is a natural phenomenon of swamp and bog gasses that seep up through the Earth and are blue in color like the flame of a pilot light. Scottish lore says that some people would follow these lights, thinking they were little fairies. The production team took this myth and created the will o' the wisps in *Brave*. The will o' the wisps light a path and beckon Merida into the forest, leading her to change her fate.

The Blue Umbrella, 2013

PARAPLUIE CAFÉ COCOA

Drink | YIELD: 2 servings | Vegetarian, Gluten Free

Sometimes you need a little push to find your path. For two lucky umbrellas (or *parapluies* in French), an entire city is on their side, ready to help them make a connection. Traffic signals, subway signs, and a particularly motivated drain nudge the protagonists of *The Blue Umbrella* together until they finally meet up at a charming sidewalk cafe. Inspired by this rainy-day tale, Parapluie Café Cocoa is a French-style hot chocolate. It's sweet, creamy, and perfect for sharing with a new friend on a drizzly afternoon.

1½ cups whole milk

½ cup heavy cream

8 ounces semisweet chocolate

2 tablespoons brown sugar

½ teaspoon vanilla extract

Whipped cream and chocolate shavings, for garnish

Heat the milk and cream in a small saucepan over medium-low heat.

Break the chocolate into small pieces and add the chocolate and brown sugar to the saucepan. Let simmer for 2 to 3 minutes, stirring constantly, until sugar is dissolved, chocolate is melted, and the hot chocolate has thickened.

Remove from the heat and mix in the vanilla extract.

Pour into 2 to-go cups and top with whipped cream and chocolate shavings. It's the perfect thing to keep yourself and a date warm on a rainy day.

Monsters University, 2013

BE MY PAL CUPCAKES

Dessert | YIELD: 24 cupcakes | Vegetarian

College can be a monstrously good time. It's the most freedom, combined with the least responsibility, most students will ever know! But even an epic experience has its difficulties. In addition to balancing classes, homework, and study groups, the students of Monsters University must navigate the tricky social scene of Greek-life rush season. Many recruits only have one chance to get in with the cool kids, so those all-important first impressions really have to count. Luckily for Randy, he has his tried-and-true cupcakes to help him make new friends. Be My Pal Cupcakes are guaranteed to impress at any Monsters U fraternity or sorority party. After all, cupcakes are never lame . . . no matter *what* they happen to spell out on Randy's face.

CUPCAKES:

4 tablespoons instant coffee powder

1½ cups milk

2 cups all-purpose flour

2 cups granulated sugar

1 cup unsweetened cocoa powder

1 teaspoon baking soda

1 teaspoon baking powder

½ teaspoon kosher salt

⅔ cup canola oil

2 teaspoons vanilla

2 eggs

TO MAKE THE CUPCAKES:

Preheat the oven to 350°F and line cupcake pans with clear or white liners.

In a small bowl, mix the instant coffee powder into the milk. Set aside.

In a large mixing bowl, sift together the flour, sugar, cocoa powder, baking soda, baking powder, and salt. Add the milk mixture, oil, and vanilla.

Mix on low speed until combined, then mix on medium speed for 2 minutes. Add the eggs one at a time and mix for 2 minutes more.

Pour the batter into the cupcake pans, filling each liner ½ full.

Bake for 22 minutes or until a toothpick inserted comes out clean. Let cool in the pans for 5 minutes and then move to racks to cool fully.

BUTTERCREAM FROSTING:

1½ cups unsalted butter

3 cups powdered sugar

1 teaspoon vanilla

Dash of kosher salt

TOPPING:

Red decorating icing

TO MAKE THE BUTTERCREAM FROSTING:

Beat the unsalted butter in the bowl of a stand mixer until light and fluffy, about 2 minutes. Slowly add the powdered sugar, ½ cup at a time, mixing fully each time. Add the vanilla and salt and mix for 2 minutes or until everything is light, fluffy, and the texture of a thick buttercream frosting. Using a butter knife or spatula, spread the frosting onto each cooled cupcake.

Write letters on each cupcake with red decorating icing to spell out "BE MY PAL."

TIP: To be accurate to the non-English-speaking versions of Monsters Inc., *draw a smiley face with glasses on the other cupcakes.*

FUN FACT

In a nod to Disney and Pixar's 2014 feature film *The Good Dinosaur*, filmmakers put a toy dinosaur on the floor of the Scare Simulator in the Scare Game's final challenge.

Lava, 2014

I LAVA YOU CAKE

Dessert | YIELD: 2 cakes | Vegetarian

Some things just take time. After all, Rome wasn't built in a day . . . and a volcano can't simply emerge overnight. But life is full of surprises. And for one lucky volcano, his perfect partner is waiting to join him when he least expects it. Modeled after that ever-hopeful volcano Uku, I Lava You Cake is a white chocolate confection with a raspberry-mango center. It's filled to the rim with gooey sweetness, and it's perfect for sharing with loved ones. *Aloha!*

FILLING:

2 tablespoons heavy cream

¼ cup (1.5 ounces) white chocolate, chopped

1 tablespoon mango purée (fresh or frozen mangos blended into a purée)

1 tablespoon raspberry purée (fresh or frozen raspberries blended into a purée)

½ teaspoon orange zest

2 drops red food coloring

CAKE:

¼ cup all-purpose flour, plus more for dusting tins

½ cup (3 ounces) white chocolate, chopped

2 tablespoons unsalted butter

2 eggs

¼ cup granulated sugar

½ teaspoon vanilla

¼ teaspoon coconut extract

⅛ teaspoon kosher salt

Powdered sugar, for dusting

SPECIAL TOOLS NEEDED:

Two 5- to 6-ounce ramekins

TO MAKE THE FILLING:

Heat the cream in a small saucepan over medium-high heat until simmering. Remove from heat and add the white chocolate, stirring until melted. Add the puréed mango and raspberry, orange zest, and food coloring. Stir until fully mixed. Pour into a pie plate or shallow bowl and refrigerate for 1 hour or until firm.

TO MAKE THE CAKES:

Preheat the oven to 350°F. Grease the ramekins, then dust flour over them, tapping out the excess. Set aside.

Heat water in the bottom of a double broiler over medium-low heat. Then add the white chocolate and butter, stirring until smooth. Set aside.

Beat the eggs, sugar, vanilla, coconut extract, and salt together in the bowl of a stand mixer until light and fluffy, scraping down the bowl halfway through.

Add the chocolate/butter mixture and mix again.

Mix in the flour. Scrape down the sides and mix again until everything is fully combined.

Pour into the ramekins, filling each ⅔ full.

Take the chilled filling and scoop ½ tablespoon into a ball. Place in the center of the batter in each ramekin. (The filling will sink down as the cake bakes, so no need to push it down.)

Bake for 20 to 22 minutes or until a toothpick inserted along the sides comes out clean. (The middle will have liquid in it, but it won't be jiggly.)

Let cool for 2 minutes, then run a thin knife along the edges, place a plate on top, and flip over, allowing the cakes to fall out inverted on the plate. Dust with powdered sugar and serve warm with a side of ice cream.

Inside Out, 2015

5-SECOND-RULE GRAPES

Dessert | YIELD: 1 cup grapes | Vegetarian, Vegan, Dairy Free, Gluten Free

According to Joy, it's okay to eat food that's been dropped on the ground . . . so long as it's there for less than five seconds. And these particular sugar-dusted grapes are a fun reminder of Riley's brush with gravity-induced disgust. Cold, crisp, and impossibly refreshing, this fruity treat is sure to bring a smile to even the most conflicted preteen!

1 cup red grapes
2 tablespoons granulated sugar

Rinse the grapes and place them in a freezer-safe plastic bag.

Add the sugar and shake, allowing all grapes to be coated in sugar.

Freeze the bag of grapes for at least an hour and enjoy. Just keep them off the ground!

Inside Out, 2015

CANDY TEARS

Dessert | YIELD: 100 teardrops | Vegetarian, Vegan, Dairy Free, Gluten Free

These Candy Tears are a tasty tribute to Riley's longtime companion, Bing Bong. Made with sugar and corn syrup, and offering just a hint of the chef's choice of flavors, Candy Tears remind us all that even in life's hard moments, there can always be a touch of sweetness.

1½ cups sugar

¾ cup light corn syrup

½ cup water

1 teaspoon citric acid

½ teaspoon liquid fruit flavoring of your choice

Liquid food coloring of your choice

½ cup powdered sugar, plus more for dusting

SPECIAL TOOLS NEEDED:

Candy thermometer

Line a rimmed baking sheet with parchment paper or aluminum foil and spray with oil. Set aside.

In a medium saucepan, mix the sugar, corn syrup, and water. Bring to a boil over medium heat and then cover with a lid for 2 minutes.

Remove the lid and continue to cook on high without stirring until a candy thermometer in the mixture reads 300°F, about 10 minutes. Add the citric acid, fruit flavoring, and food coloring and give a quick mix.

Pour the mixture onto the prepared baking sheet, spreading it evenly across the full sheet.

Let cool for 5 minutes, or until you can safely touch it with your hands, and roll the mixture toward the center of the pan. Continue doing this until the mixture stops spreading and begins to form a rope.

Spread powdered sugar over a cutting board, then place the rope on the board, stretching and rolling it until the rope is 1 inch in diameter. Cut ½-inch slices, forming each slice into a teardrop shape.

Place the powdered sugar onto a plate and roll the teardrops in the sugar, covering them.

Note:
Making candy requires precise temperatures, and cook times will vary based on the size of your pot or the strength of your stove. Please watch it carefully and use a candy thermometer to monitor the temperature.

FUN FACT

Richard Kind voices Riley's long-lost imaginary friend Bing Bong—who's made out of cotton candy. "He has a nougat-y center, which we never really see," says director Pete Docter, "and shape-wise he's part cat, part elephant, and—according to him—part dolphin. He's basically an amalgam of all the things we loved as kids."

Inside Out, 2015

BROCCOLI PIZZA

Entrée | YIELD: 1 large pizza | Vegetarian, Gluten Free

San Francisco is known throughout the world for its unique California cuisine. From fish tacos to gluten-free bakeries, it's a hub for health-conscious gastronomes. When Minnesota transplant Riley finds herself in the City by the Bay, she quickly discovers her old home and her new home have very different ideas of what constitutes a great pizza. But contrary to what Anger may think, San Francisco has most definitely not ruined pizza. Rather, Broccoli Pizza offers a healthy twist on a classic family favorite! With a gluten-free thin crust, garlic-oil sauce, and plenty of greens, this dish is sure to bring plenty of Joy to anyone who tries it . . . even Anger.

GARLIC OIL:

2 cloves garlic, peeled

2 tablespoons olive oil

PIZZA DOUGH:

¾ teaspoon active dry yeast

⅓ cup warm water

1 cup gluten-free flour

½ teaspoon kosher salt

½ teaspoon baking powder

2 tablespoons olive oil

TO MAKE THE GARLIC OIL:

Place garlic cloves and oil in a small bowl. Set aside to infuse while you make the pizza dough.

TO MAKE THE DOUGH:

Preheat the oven to 450°F and line a pizza pan or other large baking sheet with parchment paper.

Mix the yeast and water in a large bowl. Let sit for 5 minutes or until foamy.

Add the flour, salt, baking powder, and olive oil to the bowl, and combine into a dough. If too dry, add water 1 tablespoon at a time. If too wet, add flour 1 tablespoon at a time.

Form the dough into a disc and place on a floured surface. Cover with a clean kitchen towel and let rest for 30 minutes.

TOPPINGS:

¼ cup broccoli, cut into small florets

¼ zucchini, cut into half-moon slices

1 tablespoon olive oil

⅛ teaspoon salt

⅛ teaspoon freshly ground black pepper

6 ounces whole milk low-moisture mozzarella, shredded

3 cloves garlic, cut into slices

¼ cup fresh spinach leaves

SPECIAL TOOLS NEEDED:

Pizza pan (or large baking sheet)

Cutting board

Pizza cutter, mezzaluna, or large knife

TO PREPARE THE TOPPINGS:

While the dough is resting, roast the veggies. Place the broccoli and zucchini on a baking sheet lined with parchment paper and drizzle the olive oil over the veggies. Top with salt and pepper, and roast for 10 minutes. Remove from the oven and set aside.

TO MAKE THE PIZZA:

Place the rested dough between two oiled sheets of parchment paper and roll out into a 12-inch circle. Brush the garlic-infused olive oil over top, leaving a ½ inch edge free of oil for the crust.

Sprinkle cheese evenly on top of the oil, and then top with the roasted veggies, garlic, and spinach.

Bake for 8 to 10 minutes, or until the cheese is melted and crust is crisp.

Remove the pizza from the oven and onto a cutting board. Let sit for a few minutes and cut into 8 pieces.

FUN FACT

John Ratzenberger, who has voiced a character in nearly all of Pixar's feature films, provides the voice of Mind Worker Fritz in *Inside Out*.

Inside Out, 2015

BRAIN FREEZE

Drink | YIELD: 4 servings | Vegetarian, Vegan, Dairy Free, Gluten Free

Riley is all too familiar with the chilling moment that comes right after taking a big bite of ice cream or a slurp of a cold drink. This Brain Freeze drink, inspired by that highly relatable moment, evokes that chilly sensation . . . but with a tasty twist. It's a made-to-order slushie that utilizes tinted drink mix to match the chef's emotion of the day—yellow for Joy, blue for Sadness, red for Anger, purple for Fear, and green should its maker feel a particular amount of Disgust. Brain Freeze is an instant mood lifter that's perfect for sharing with friends old and new.

2 cups club soda

½ cup granulated sugar

½ teaspoon powdered drink mix (like Kool-Aid) in the color of your emotions today (yellow for Joy, blue for Sadness, red for Anger, purple for Fear, and green for Disgust)

4 cups ice

Place the club soda, sugar, and drink mix into a blender.

Top with 2 cups ice and blend for 30 seconds.

Add the rest of the ice and blend for another 30 seconds or until it has a smooth, consistent texture.

Pour into 4 glasses.

SPECIAL TOOLS NEEDED:

Blender

The Good Dinosaur, 2015

ANCIENT GRAINS AND CORN SALAD

Appetizer | YIELD: 2 salads | Vegetarian, Gluten Free

Ancient foods like quinoa and barley are healthful grains that have been around since before the dinosaurs roamed the earth—and a certain Apatosaurus family opened their farm! These grains offer impressive dietary benefits, and taste downright delicious when cooked with vegetable broth and tossed in a dressing that blends lime juice with just a hint of honey! Topped with cheddar cheese and avocado slices, this Ancient Grains and Corn Salad is a protein-packed meal that's fit for a modern-day dinosaur.

⅓ cup quinoa, dry

⅓ cup millet, dry

2 cups vegetable broth

1½ teaspoons kosher salt, divided

2 tablespoons olive oil

1 tablespoon lime juice

½ tablespoon honey

1 teaspoon Dijon mustard

¼ teaspoon freshly ground black pepper

Dash of garlic powder

1 cup dinosaur kale

¼ red onion, sliced

½ cup frozen corn, thawed (or fresh, cooked and cut off the cob)

¼ cup white cheddar, diced

6 cherry tomatoes, sliced

½ avocado, sliced

Bring the quinoa, millet, broth, and 1 teaspoon of salt to a boil in a medium saucepan over medium-high heat. Reduce to low, bringing the grains to a simmer, cover, and cook for 15 minutes or until liquid is absorbed and grains are tender. Fluff the grains with a fork and set aside to cool.

In a small bowl, whisk together the olive oil, lime juice, honey, mustard, remaining ½ teaspoon salt, pepper, and garlic powder to make the dressing. Set aside.

Rinse and rip the dinosaur kale into small pieces and place in a large bowl. Top with the quinoa mixture, onion, corn, cheddar cheese, and tomatoes. Toss with the dressing. Divide the salad up between two bowls and garnish with slices of avocado.

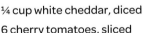

FUN FACT

Inspired by the American Northwest, the setting for *The Good Dinosaur* is not only completely outside, it features ever-changing weather. To prepare, Pixar's artists and technicians created a rain and cloud library, featuring different types of rain and a selection of clouds that could be mixed and matched, and stretched, squashed, and manipulated to create any desired look. Although clouds are typically done in matte paintings, for the first time ever, *The Good Dinosaur* features 100-percent volumetric clouds. This means they are mobile, dimensional, and can be lit from any camera angle, creating a stunning look.

The Good Dinosaur, 2015

BERRY BOARD

Dessert | YIELD: 1 board or 8 servings | Vegetarian

A good charcuterie board is timeless. After all, who wouldn't enjoy a board made up of nuts, berries, and the perennial favorite, dark chocolate? This Berry Board, inspired by the wondrous world of *The Good Dinosaur,* will be equally at home at a picnic, in a formal gathering, or even in a cave. It's a much-loved platter that's sure to please any diner— even those who find themselves living on the wild side.

12 ounces dark chocolate

¼ cup dried cherries

¼ cup pistachios

1 pomegranate

2 plums

1 small bunch grapes

6 chocolate wafer straws

1 pint raspberries

1 pint blueberries

½ cup candy rocks

6 mint leaves

SPECIAL TOOLS NEEDED:

Large wood board

Double boiler

Melt the chocolate in a double boiler or 30 seconds at a time in the microwave and pour onto a parchment paper–lined baking sheet, spreading it evenly, no more than ¼ inch thick. Sprinkle the dried cherries and pistachios on top and let harden for 15 minutes in the fridge or a couple hours at room temperature. Once hardened, break the chocolate into jagged pieces of "bark."

Scatter the bark onto the large wood board.

Break a pomegranate open and place it on the board with its seeds spilling out.

Cut the plums in half, remove the pits, and place the halves around the board. Place the grapes on the board.

Fan out 3 chocolate wafer straws on each side of the board.

Fill out the rest of the board with the raspberries, blueberries, and candy rocks. Accent with mint leaves.

FUN FACT

The Good Dinosaur features more water shots than any Pixar feature before it, including more than 125 shots of the river alone.

Finding Dory, 2016

DORY'S PURPLE SHELLS

Dessert | YIELD: 20 shells | Vegetarian

The adorable little fish Dory has a soft spot for shells. They're shiny, soothing, and they can be arranged into trails to help a forgetful little fish find her way home! Dory's Purple Shells are a culinary nod to the Blue Tang's beloved parents. With vanilla, sugar, and a zesty pop of lemon, these cake-like cookies will quickly become a household staple. Just keep swimming . . . and baking!

½ cup unsalted butter

2 eggs

½ cup granulated sugar

1 teaspoon lemon zest

1 teaspoon vanilla

Purple gel food coloring

1 cup all-purpose flour

½ teaspoon baking powder

⅛ teaspoon kosher salt

SPECIAL TOOLS NEEDED:

Madeleine pan

Melt the butter by microwaving in a small bowl for 30 seconds, stirring, and repeating until fully melted. Set aside.

Beat the eggs and sugar on high in the bowl of a stand mixer with a whisk attachment. Continue beating for 8 minutes or until the mixture is thick and pale. Add in the lemon zest, vanilla, and a few drops of purple food coloring, and mix until combined. If the color is not accurate, add another drop or two and mix again.

In a separate small bowl, mix the flour, baking powder, and salt. Gently fold the flour mixture into the wet mixture.

Add the (slightly cooled) melted butter into the batter and stir until smooth and shiny.

Chill the batter in the fridge for 30 minutes, and preheat the oven to 350°F.

Grease and flour a madeleine pan and spoon 1 tablespoon batter into the middle of each cavity.

Bake for 8 to 10 minutes or until the madeleines spring back slightly when touched.

Invert the pan to remove the madeleines and let cool on a wire rack. Repeat steps 6 through 8 with any remaining batter.

FUN FACT

The iconic Pizza Planet truck can be seen among debris in the shipping lanes that Dory, Marlin, and Nemo pass through on their way to the Marine Life Institute.

MOVIE SPOTLIGHT:
COCO

Memorable Quote: "Nothing's more important than family."

Release Year: 2017

Directors: Lee Unkrich and Adrian Molina

In *Coco*, twelve-year-old Miguel Rivera dreams of becoming a musician. But his family has banished music from their home, leaving Miguel to pursue his passion in secret. On Día de los Muertos, Miguel borrows the guitar on the famed singer Ernesto de la Cruz's grave . . . and sets in motion a series of events that reunites him with lost relatives, while healing old wounds in the most unexpected of ways. This beautiful account of intergenerational relationships and the importance of honoring family while carving one's own way in the world was an immediate hit with audiences around the world. It received two Academy Awards—for Best Animated Feature and Best Original Song for "Remember Me"—and it remains a beloved classic in households across the globe.

Coco beautifully demonstrates the strength of family ties, and the ways in which we can honor our loved ones—both living and dead—through sharing their stories, crafting *ofrendas*, and of course, making their favorite meals. Food lies at the heart of the Rivera family, with Miguel and his relatives coming together around the table to tell tales, ease worries, and of course, enjoy the shared meals that fuel them throughout their many adventures. Miguel quickly learns that he should *never* turn down his *abuelita's* tamales—no matter how full his plate already is! After all, his grandmother shares her love through cooking—a fact that proves especially helpful on Día de los Muertos, when the Riveras prepare food to place at the *ofrendas* of their departed relatives. The family works together to make *pan de muerto*—a popular Mexican sweet bread—along with loved ones' favorite meals, which they lovingly place alongside a display of candles, apples, and sugar skulls. Food brings Miguel's family together—and solidifies their ties to relatives who have crossed the Marigold Bridge. It's a living reminder that so long as we remember those who have passed, they are never truly gone.

In animating *Coco*, filmmakers wanted to be as authentic as possible. To accurately create Miguel's Xoloitzcuintli companion, Dante, they brought in local Xolo dogs for the artists to study . . . and to play with! And during their research trips to Mexico, *Coco's* creators learned that during Día de los Muertos, the scent and shade of marigolds is believed to guide spirits home to their families. Accordingly, they used a multitude of marigolds to decorate the Land of the Dead, as well as the *ofrendas* in the land of the living. With its attention to detail, moving musicality, and focus on this most unusual—yet ever-relatable—family, *Coco* has more than earned its place amongst Pixar's most beloved films. As Ernesto says, "One cannot deny who one is meant to be." And it's abundantly clear that *Coco* is meant to become a classic. *Salud!*

Coco, 2017

PAN DE MUERTO

Dessert | YIELD: 1 loaf of bread | Vegetarian

Every fall, the Rivera family honors their ancestors by cooking up a batch of sweet rolls. This version of Pan de Muerto offers a zesty twist on that special family recipe, by adding just a touch of orange to the traditional flour dough. And while a certain Rivera relative knows that one should never underestimate the power of music, these rolls will prove every bit as adept at bridging divides, healing old wounds, and bringing families together.

BREAD:

¼ cup milk

¼ cup unsalted butter

¼ cup water

¼ cup granulated sugar

1 teaspoon ground star anise

1 packet (2¼ teaspoons) active dry yeast

½ teaspoon kosher salt

Zest from 2 oranges

2 eggs

3 cups all-purpose flour

GLAZE:

Juice from the zested oranges, freshly squeezed

1 cup granulated sugar, divided

TO MAKE THE BREAD:

Heat the milk, butter, and water in a small saucepan over low heat just until the butter melts, stirring often. Temperature should be around 110°F (not hot enough to burn you). Set aside.

In a large mixing bowl, with a bread hook attachment, mix the sugar, star anise, yeast, salt, and orange zest. Slowly add in the liquid, mixing on low just until combined. Add in the eggs one at a time, mixing fully in between. Slowly add in the flour while mixing on low, and then mix on medium for 1 minute or until dough is fully combined and soft.

Knead the dough on a floured surface until smooth and elastic. Place in a lightly greased bowl and cover with plastic wrap. Let rise until doubled in size, about 1 to 2 hours.

On a floured surface, punch down the loaf and cut off ¼ of the dough. Shape the remaining dough into a large round loaf. With the ¼ dough, form two long ropes (lengths should match the diameter of the loaf), four small knobs (about 1 inch each), and one large knob (about 2 inches). Place the smaller knobs on the ends of each rope, to make them look like bones. Place the "bones" on the top of the loaf in a cross pattern. Place the larger knob in the center, on top of the "bones."

Cover the loaf loosely with plastic wrap, and allow it to rise again for 1 hour.

Preheat the oven to 350°F and bake for 35 to 45 minutes or until golden brown.

TO MAKE THE GLAZE:

Let bread cool while you make the glaze: Juice the two oranges and strain the pulp out. Bring the juice and ¾ cup sugar to a boil in a small saucepan over high heat, stirring often. Reduce heat to low and let simmer for 2 minutes, or until sugar has dissolved and the juice has reduced. Let cool.

Brush the glaze over the top of the bread and sprinkle with the remaining ¼ cup sugar, covering the entire top.

FUN FACT

Artists at Pixar Animation Studios like to add vegetation—grass, trees, bushes—to exterior environments. But *Coco* filmmakers felt the Land of the Dead should be different. The only living plants in the vibrant fantastical world are marigolds.

Coco, 2017

ABUELITA'S TAMALES

Entrée | YIELD: 20 tamales | Dairy Free, Gluten Free

Never say no to your grandmother—especially when she's offering food! Miguel quickly learns to graciously accept his grandmother's offerings, despite having an already full plate. After all, Abuelita's Tamales are a Rivera family classic. And this pork tamale recipe, inspired by the beloved matriarch, is sure to have everyone clamoring for more. Salty, savory, and nostalgic, Abuelita's Tamales evoke all the feelings of love and security that come from sharing a meal with loved ones—from both sides of the Marigold Bridge.

PORK FILLING:

2½ pounds pork shoulder or pork butt, cut into 3-inch pieces

6 cups water

1 onion, quartered

3 cloves garlic, minced

2 teaspoons kosher salt

1 teaspoon freshly ground black pepper

1 bay leaf

1 package dried corn husks (will need about 20 individual husks)

SAUCE:

3 tablespoons canola oil

2 tablespoons all-purpose flour

1½ tablespoons chili powder

½ teaspoon cumin

½ teaspoon garlic powder

½ teaspoon kosher salt

8 ounces tomato sauce

1½ cups vegetable broth

TO MAKE THE PORK FILLING:

Fill a large Dutch oven or pot with the pork, water, onion, garlic, salt, pepper, and bay leaf. Bring to a boil over high heat and then simmer on low uncovered for 90 minutes, or until the pork is tender and can easily shred with a fork.

While the pork is cooking, start to soak the husks: Place the corn husks in a large bowl and cover with warm water. Soak for 30 minutes or until husks are softened.

TO MAKE THE SAUCE:

Heat the canola oil in a small saucepan over medium heat and then whisk in the flour for 1 minute. Add the chili powder, ½ teaspoon of cumin, garlic, and ½ teaspoon of salt, and whisk for 1 additional minute. Whisk in the tomato sauce and vegetable broth, then simmer on low heat for 10 minutes or until sauce is thickened.

Remove the pork from the broth and let cool. Strain and reserve 2 cups of the broth for later. Once cooled, discard any fat and shred the pork using two forks. Mix the pork with the red sauce and set aside.

DOUGH:

⅔ cup lard (or shortening)

2 cups masa harina

1 teaspoon baking powder

½ teaspoon kosher salt

½ teaspoon cumin

SPECIAL TOOLS NEEDED:

Steamer

TO MAKE THE DOUGH:

Mix the lard and 1 tablespoon of the reserved pork broth together in the bowl of a stand mixer and mix until fluffy. Add the masa harina, baking powder, salt, and cumin, and mix. Slowly add in the rest of broth (totaling 2 cups) while mixing on low. Increase the mixing speed to medium and mix for 10 minutes or until the dough is fluffy and spongy, occasionally stopping to scrape the sides of the bowl.

Remove the husks from the water if you haven't already and let sit on a paper towel. Taking one husk at a time, spread approximately 3 tablespoons dough onto the husk, making a 3- to 4-inch square about ¼ inch thick.

Place 1½ tablespoons of the pork filling in a line in the center of the dough square. Fold the husk vertically, closing the masa dough over the filling. Fold over the additional vertical husk edge, and then fold up the top and bottom parts of the husk, as if making a burrito. Continue with the rest of the tamales.

Lay additional corn husks on the bottom of a steamer rack and place the tamales in the steamer, standing upright. Place soaked corn husks or a wet towel on the top of the tamales, and cover with a lid.

Bring the steamer water to boiling over high heat, then reduce heat to low to simmer and steam for 45 to 60 minutes. Tamales are done when the husk pulls away from the tamale easily.

Let sit for 10 minutes to help them stiffen up, then remove the husk and enjoy.

FUN FACT

Miguel's loyal canine companion Dante is a Xolo dog—short for Xoloitzcuintli—the national dog of Mexico, whose origins are deeply rooted in Mesoamerican civilization. The Xolo was regarded as the representative on Earth of the Aztec god Xolotl, the god of fire and lightning. Nearly hairless, Xolos also often have missing teeth, and for that reason, their tongue naturally hangs out. Filmmakers wanted to include this in Dante's design and have his tongue behave like a character itself. To achieve the look, they borrowed the rig used in *Finding Dory* for "septopus" Hank's dynamic tentacles.

Bao, 2018

BONDING THROUGH BAO

Appetizer | YIELD: 36 bao | Dairy Free

Growing up can cause some tricky adjustments—not only for children, but for the parents who love them. The short film *Bao* observes this tumultuous time through the lens of a longstanding Chinese family tradition—coming together to make a beloved delicacy. The word *bao* translates to "precious" or "treasure"—which captures both the essence of the food, and the experience of crafting a meal that's meant to be shared with loved ones. And this recipe from *Bao* director Domee Shi brings together ground pork, Chinese cabbage, and oyster sauce in a wonderful blend of familiar and unexpected flavors—just like the short that inspired it.

4 cups all-purpose flour

¾ teaspoon active dry yeast

2 cups water

2 teaspoons canola oil

1 pound ground pork

1 pound Chinese cabbage, minced

1 carrot, minced

2 to 3 stalks green onion, chopped

1 teaspoon ground ginger

1 teaspoon olive oil

Freshly ground pepper, to taste

½ teaspoon chicken bouillon powder

1 teaspoon oyster sauce

2 teaspoons cooking wine

1 egg, beaten

Salt, to taste

Additional cabbage leaves for the steamer basket

SPECIAL TOOLS NEEDED:

Steamer basket

Mix the flour and yeast in a large mixing bowl.

Add the water and knead until a solid dough ball forms. If it gets too sticky, add more flour, 1 tablespoon at a time. If it's too dry, add more water, 1 tablespoon at a time.

Cover the bowl with plastic wrap and let the dough rise for 2 hours.

Heat the oil in a medium pan over medium-high heat, then add half of the ground pork. Cook until browned, about 3 minutes.

In a large bowl, mix the cooked pork and raw pork with the cabbage, carrot, green onions, ground ginger, olive oil, pepper, chicken bouillon powder, oyster sauce, cooking wine, beaten egg, and salt.

Once your dough has risen, dust your countertop with flour and roll out the dough into a long rope, using the "windmill technique." (Poke a hole through the middle of the dough, and start rotating the dough, holding onto the edges, allowing the dough to stretch out into a long rope circle. Cut one side to form a large dough rope.)

Cut the dough rope into ½-inch pieces. Roll each piece out into a circle to be used as the bao wrapper (about 3 inches in diameter).

Spoon ½ tablespoon of filling into the center of each wrapper. Then carefully pinch and fold the wrapper closed, twisting the top to finish. Make sure to press the dough tight to seal the top.

Take a pot that fits a steamer basket on top and fill it with 2 inches of water. Bring to a boil over medium-high heat. Place the baos in a steaming basket lined with cabbage leaves to prevent sticking, and place the basket on top of the boiling pot of water. Close the lid. Steam for 15 minutes, then turn off heat and let the baos rest for 5 minutes.

Eat, or adopt as your surrogate child.

Incredibles 2, 2018

BREAKFAST OF SUPERS

Entrée | YIELD: 8 waffles | Vegetarian

Supers need a solid breakfast. After all, it takes a lot of energy to save the world. And there's no better way to kick off a super day than with lightly sweetened, high-protein waffles. Two kinds of flour, Greek yogurt, and almond milk come together to create a powerful burst of flavor. Breakfast of Supers is so good, it should be illegal . . . just like the Supers who eat it!

1 cup whole wheat flour

1 cup almond flour

2 tablespoons granulated sugar

1 teaspoon baking powder

1 teaspoon kosher salt

½ teaspoon baking soda

½ teaspoon cinnamon

1 cup vanilla Greek yogurt

1 cup almond milk

4 eggs

6 tablespoons unsalted butter, melted

1 teaspoon vanilla

Cooking spray or butter for waffle iron (if needed)

Almond butter

Cinnamon

Fruit (bananas, berries, and/or thinly sliced apples or pears)

SPECIAL TOOLS NEEDED:

Waffle maker

Mix the whole wheat flour, almond flour, sugar, baking powder, salt, baking soda, and cinnamon in a medium bowl. Set aside.

In a separate bowl, mix the yogurt, milk, eggs, butter, and vanilla. Slowly add in the dry ingredients and mix just until combined.

Preheat a waffle iron and coat with butter or cooking spray. Pour ½ cup of batter into the waffle iron at a time, cooking until golden brown. Repeat until all batter is gone.

Top with almond butter, cinnamon, and fruit.

Note:
Total servings for this recipe may vary based on the waffle maker used.

JACK-JACK'S COOKIE NUM-NUM

Dessert | YIELD: 8 large cookies | Vegetarian

Jack-Jack may be the Parr family's littlest Super . . . but the tiny tyke is coming into some very big powers. He's primarily a polymorph, but he can also move through solid objects, self-duplicate, and even burst into flames. And just like Jack-Jack himself, Jack-Jack's Cookie Num-Num brings unexpected ingredients together in one singularly spectacular treat. With mix-ins that range from potato chips to popping candy, super chefs will have an array of choices when crafting their very own signature, super-sized cookie.

1 cup salted butter

1 cup brown sugar

½ cup granulated sugar

2 eggs

1 teaspoon vanilla

2½ cups all-purpose flour

1 teaspoon salt

¾ teaspoon baking soda

⅓ cup each of 5 of the following mix-ins of your choice:

Chocolate chips

Butterscotch chips

Nuts

Oats

Raisins

Potato chips

Pretzels

Pop Rocks

M&Ms

Coconut

SPECIAL TOOLS NEEDED:

2¾-inch cookie dough scoop

Mix the butter in the bowl of a stand mixer or a large bowl until it is light and creamy, then mix in the brown and granulated sugars.

One at a time, add in the eggs, and the vanilla, mixing fully in between each addition.

Mix the flour, salt, and baking soda together in a separate large bowl, and then slowly add into the wet mixture until everything is fully mixed.

Stir in the mix-ins of your choice.

Cover the top of the bowl of cookie dough with plastic wrap and refrigerate for 1 hour.

Fifteen minutes before the cookie dough comes out of the fridge, preheat the oven to 375°F. Cover two large cookie sheets with parchment paper.

Using a large cookie scoop, drop round balls of cookie dough onto the cookie sheets, 2 inches apart from each other.

Bake for 15 minutes, or until the edges of the cookies are light brown, and the cookies are firm but still slightly doughy.

Cool for 5 minutes and then transfer to a wire rack to finish cooling.

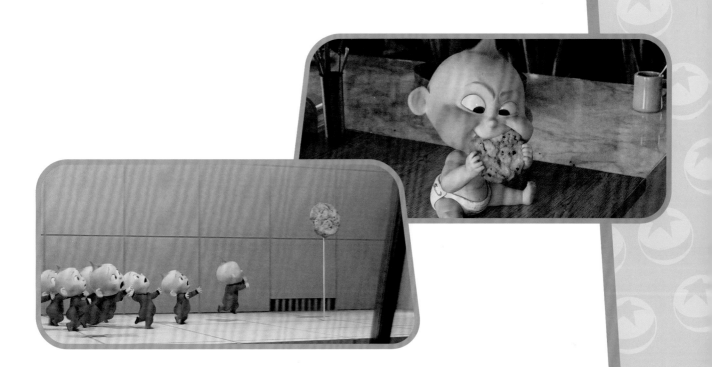

Director Brad Bird was more interested in the characters than their superpowers: "I decided to base the powers on the personalities of the characters. Traditionally, the father is the strong one in the family, so Bob's power is super strength. Helen as wife and mother is being pulled in many different directions, so she seemed to be somebody who could stretch and contort without breaking. Violet is an insecure teenage girl who doesn't want people to look at her, so she gets to become invisible, and because she's a little insulated and protective, she can project this force field. Young boys are hyperactive and have enough energy to power a small village, so I decided to make Dash really fast. The baby, Jack-Jack, has no known powers, so he's all unformed potential."

Incredibles 2, 2018

THE HAPPY PLATTER SURPRISE

Entrée | YIELD: 4 servings

All parents (even Super ones!) know that parenting is a heroic act—when done properly. Sometimes that act requires the valiant task of learning new math. And other times, it may call for a special trip to the workplace of their daughter's memory-wiped crush. Either way, Bob and Helen Parr know that the best means of ensuring the whole family has a positively super day is with a hearty meal. This fun option from the ever-popular Happy Platter menu calls upon the tried-and-true ingredients of a much-loved American classic. Perfectly seasoned chicken-fried steak, rich gravy, and a light vegetable side ensure that Supers both big and small get all the nutrients they need to spend the day using their powers for good. And thanks to its rich bounty of colors and flavors, this particular platter is anything but boring. In fact, it's downright . . . *happy*!

CHICKEN-FRIED STEAK:

½ cup all-purpose flour

2 teaspoons kosher salt

1½ teaspoons garlic powder

½ teaspoon cayenne pepper

2 large eggs

2 tablespoons whole milk

¼ cup canola oil

4 cube steaks (about ⅓ pound each)

½ teaspoon kosher salt

¼ teaspoon freshly ground black pepper

GRAVY:

3 tablespoons all-purpose flour

2 cups whole milk

½ teaspoon kosher salt

¼ teaspoon freshly ground black pepper

GREEN BEANS:

1 tablespoon plus 1 teaspoon kosher salt, divided

1 pound fresh green beans, trimmed

4 slices bacon

½ medium yellow onion, diced

2 cloves garlic, minced

½ teaspoon freshly ground black pepper

TO MAKE THE STEAKS:

Mix the flour, salt, garlic powder, and cayenne pepper together in a medium bowl and then place the mixture on a large plate. Set aside.

Whisk the eggs and milk together in a small bowl. Set aside.

Preheat a large pan on the stove over medium heat. Once heated, add the canola oil, fully covering the bottom of the pan.

Salt and pepper the steaks, then dip them into the flour mixture, coating them. Then, dip them in the whisked egg mixture. Finally, dip them back into the flour mixture, fully coating both sides of the steaks.

Carefully place the steaks into the pan and cook for 2 minutes on each side. (You may need to cook the steaks in batches.) The steak and coating will begin to look golden brown.

Place the steaks on a paper towel–lined plate and cover loosely with aluminum foil to keep in the heat.

TO MAKE THE GRAVY:

Without cleaning out the grease in the pan, add the flour, whisking often, to make a roux.

Once the roux is a golden brown color, slowly pour in the milk, whisking constantly. Add salt and pepper, and cook, whisking often, for 5 to 10 minutes or until thick.

TO MAKE THE GREEN BEANS:

Boil a large pot of water and 1 tablespoon of kosher salt. Add the green beans and cook uncovered for 5 minutes or until green beans are crisp-tender. Drain and set the beans aside.

Place bacon in a large pan over medium heat and cook for 3 minutes on one side, then 2 minutes on the other, or until bacon is crispy. Remove the bacon to a paper towel–lined plate, and when cooled, crumble.

Keeping the bacon grease in the pan, add the diced onion and garlic and let cook for 1 minute or until fragrant. Add the green beans back to the pan, add the teaspoon of kosher salt and the black pepper, and cook for 2 to 3 minutes or until everything is warmed and mixed together. Stir in half of the crumbled bacon, and reserve the other half to sprinkle on top of the beans when serving.

Plate the steak, pour gravy on top, and serve with green beans topped with bacon crumbles on the side.

CHAPTER FOUR
THE LEGACY CONTINUES

2020-TODAY

Onward, 2020

THE MANTICORE'S TAVERN SOUP OF THE DAY

Appetizer | YIELD: 6 bowls of stew | Dairy Free

As New Mushroomton's go-to family restaurant, the Manticore's Tavern offers a Fun Zone, a storied history, and of course, a wide array of delicious dishes. And the tavern's soup of the day is always an especially monstrous hit. With carrots, potato, and onion, this replica of the tavern's hearty beef stew is the perfect way to fuel up before embarking on an epic quest . . . or a spirited family game night!

¼ cup all-purpose flour

1½ teaspoons kosher salt, divided

1 teaspoon freshly ground black pepper, divided

2 pounds beef stew meat, cut into 1-inch cubes

1 to 3 tablespoons olive oil, depending on batches of stew meat

1 yellow onion, chopped

3 potatoes, diced

4 carrots, sliced

2 cups beef broth

1 tablespoon Worcestershire sauce

4 cloves garlic, minced

1 bay leaf

1 teaspoon paprika

1 teaspoon thyme

In a large bowl, mix the flour, ½ teaspoon salt, and ½ teaspoon pepper. Mix in the meat until it's all evenly coated in the flour mixture.

Cook the meat over medium-high heat in a large skillet with 1 tablespoon olive oil for 1 minute on each side or until slightly browned. (You may need to do this in batches to avoid overcrowding.) Place the meat into a slow cooker.

Add in the onion, potatoes, carrots, beef broth, Worcestershire sauce, garlic, bay leaf, paprika, thyme, and the 1 teaspoon salt and remaining ½ teaspoon pepper.

Cover and cook on low for 10 to 12 hours, or on high for 4 to 6 hours, stirring occasionally. The stew is done when beef is fully browned and vegetables are tender.

FUN FACT

Onward reflects the modern world, including characters reflective of various dimensions of ability and diversity. Students speak in American Sign Language behind Ian (they sign "Boy, cute" unbeknownst to him). In the scene at Burger Shire, a pedestrian who is visually impaired enlists the help of a service dragon. Additionally, in Manticore's Tavern, an elderly elf dons a hearing aid, and a teenage satyr navigates a wheelchair.

Onward, 2020

BURGER SHIRE SECOND BREAKFAST SANDWICH

Entrée | YIELD: 1 sandwich

The fast-food chain Burger Shire is known for its quick and easy meals. From greasy burgers to salty fries, it's a favorite of brothers Ian and Barley Lightfoot. In addition to its regular offerings, Burger Shire is now serving second breakfast—something everyone can enjoy, thanks to this *Onward*-inspired recipe! A Burger Shire Second Breakfast Sandwich brings eggs, sausage, and Muenster cheese together within a pretzel bun, creating a savory meal that's easily transportable—no van required.

1 sausage patty

2 eggs

1 tablespoon milk

Dash of salt

Dash of pepper

1 Pretzel bun

½ teaspoon mayonnaise

½ teaspoon Dijon mustard

1 slice Muenster cheese

¼ cup arugula, loosely packed

SPECIAL TOOLS NEEDED:

Egg ring

Heat a small nonstick pan over medium heat and add the sausage patty (add 1 tablespoon of oil if your sausage is particularly lean). Cook 3 minutes on each side, or until fully warmed, browned, and slightly crispy. Set aside.

Crack the eggs in a small bowl and add the milk, salt, and pepper. Whisk until fully mixed.

To give the eggs the perfect fast food–restaurant look, cook the eggs in a round egg ring. In the same nonstick pan on medium heat, scramble the eggs for 2 to 3 minutes or until solidified, using the grease from the sausage.

While the eggs are cooking, toast your bun to desired brownness.

Spread the mayonnaise on one side of the bun, and mustard on the other. Place the sausage patty on the bottom, followed by the egg, the slice of cheese, and the arugula. Top with the other side of the bun.

FUN FACT

To create reference footage that would help animators realize a pair of pants as a character, filmmakers donned green suits, khakis, and a pair of shoes. With their arms tied behind their backs, they danced around a mo-cap stage and stumbled up and down boxes. Later, they were able to digitally remove their upper bodies thanks to movie magic and get a good idea how a pair of pants might move.

Onward, 2020

BARLEY'S FAVORITE CHEESE PUFFS

Snack | YIELD: About 40 cheese puffs | Vegetarian

A day of questing can leave anyone tired . . . not to mention peckish! And for the residents of New Mushroomton, Barley's Favorite Cheese Puffs offer the perfect, individually wrapped pick-me-up to get them through their next big adventure. This homemade recipe is every bit as delightful as the packaged variety. Made with milk, cheese powder, and in a nod to its original manufacturer, Gorgonzola cheese, these treats will have anyone believing in magic.

4 tablespoons salted butter

1 teaspoon kosher salt, divided

⅛ teaspoon garlic powder

1 cup all-purpose flour

1½ teaspoons cornmeal

1 cup Gorgonzola cheese, crumbled

¾ cup milk

4 cups canola oil

2 tablespoons cheese powder

½ teaspoon buttermilk powder

¼ teaspoon cornstarch

Beat the butter, ½ teaspoon salt, and garlic powder in the bowl of a stand mixer for 1 to 2 minutes or until the butter is light and fluffy.

Scrape down the sides of the mixing bowl with a spatula, and add the flour, cornmeal, and Gorgonzola cheese. Mix until combined. Slowly add in the milk, mixing until a thick batter forms.

Heat canola oil in a Dutch oven or heavy-bottomed pan over high heat until it reaches 400°F.

While waiting for the oil to heat, mix the cheese powder, buttermilk powder, remaining ½ teaspoon salt, and cornstarch in a small bowl. Set aside. Place paper towels onto a large plate. Set aside.

Place the batter in a piping bag or a zippered bag with the corner cut off, and pipe chunks of dough into the hot oil. Let fry about 20 to 30 seconds per side, until the puffs are evenly dark brown and crispy.

Drain the fried puffs on the paper towel–lined plate and toss with the seasoning mixture. Continue with the rest of the batter, and let the puffs cool.

FUN FACT

Artists charged with designing Ian's bedroom wanted to leave subtle hints as to his personality. One poster features a fictional band called the Chanterelles— named for the mushroom-shaped houses in the film. There are also astronomy posters and a few photos that are actually stills from *The Good Dinosaur*.

MANTICORE'S TAVERN ROAST BEAST

Entrée | YIELD: 6 servings | Dairy Free, Gluten Free

As a seasoned warrior, the Manticore knows that adventure requires a certain degree of risk-taking. And after a lifetime of questing, she now prides herself on running her beloved restaurant, the Manticore's Tavern. Her family-friendly menu offers something for everyone—from the pickiest eater to the ultimate epicurean. Inspired by one of her most popular dishes, Manticore's Tavern Roast Beast is a flavor-packed favorite. Served with an array of vegetables and seasoned with dry rub (with an optional barbeque dip on the side!), this hearty dish is designed to bring out the inner warrior in anyone.

3 tablespoons brown sugar

1 tablespoon garlic powder

1 tablespoon plus 1 teaspoon kosher salt, divided

2 teaspoons onion powder

2 teaspoons smoked paprika

½ teaspoon freshly ground black pepper, divided

One 3-pound beef rump or round roast

4 tablespoon olive oil, divided

16 ounces small red potatoes, quartered

8 ounces baby carrots

4 ounces mushrooms

3 tablespoons olive oil for the vegetables

Barbecue sauce, for dipping (optional)

SPECIAL TOOLS NEEDED:

Meat thermometer

Preheat the oven to 325°F.

In a small bowl, mix the brown sugar, garlic powder, salt, onion powder, paprika, and pepper.

Uncover the roast, cover with 1 tablespoon olive oil, and rub the spice mixture all over the outside. Place the roast on a rack inside of a roasting pan.

Place the potatoes, carrots, and mushrooms in a large bowl with the remaining 3 tablespoons olive oil, remaining teaspoon salt, and remaining teaspoon pepper. Pour the potatoes, carrots, and mushrooms into the roasting pan.

Cook in the oven for 90 minutes or until a meat thermometer reads 145°F.

Remove the roast and loosely cover with aluminum foil. Let rest for 15 minutes before slicing.

Serve a few slices of roast beef with a serving of vegetables, and include a side of barbecue sauce for dipping.

SOULFUL BAGELS

Snack | YIELD: 8 bagels | Vegetarian, Vegan, Dairy Free

Joe Gardner's life hasn't exactly gone according to plan. The talented piano player has always dreamed of becoming a successful musician, but for now, he pays the bills by teaching middle school band. Inspiring a rowdy group of preteens requires a lot of determination and a goodly amount of stamina. And because Joe knows he can't eat dreams for breakfast, he hits the streets of his hometown, the Big Apple—which happens to be the bagel capital of the world. Soulful Bagels draw on these famous New York treats—a delicacy so beloved and one which 22 once shared with a local busker to thank him for his beautiful music. And with toppings that range from shredded cheese to cinnamon sugar, these snacks can be every bit as creative as the city—and the music teacher—that inspired them. Lightly sweetened and filled with doughy goodness, Soulful Bagels are sure to have any diner asking, "Is this heaven?"

2 teaspoons active dry yeast

4½ teaspoons granulated sugar

1¼ cups warm water, divided

4 cups bread flour, divided

2 teaspoons salt, divided

2 tablespoons olive oil

1 tablespoon brown sugar or barley malt syrup

½ teaspoon baking soda

OPTIONAL TOPPINGS FOR THE BAGELS:

Everything bagel seasoning, salt, dehydrated onion, sesame seeds, shredded cheese, cinnamon sugar, or anything your mind can think of!

Mix the yeast, granulated sugar, and ½ cup of warm water in a small bowl and set aside for 5 minutes while the yeast activates.

Place 3½ cups bread flour and 1½ teaspoons salt in the bowl of a standing mixer fitted with a dough hook and give a quick mix. Add the remaining ¾ cup warm water and the activated yeast mixture and mix for 10 minutes. While it's mixing, slowly add in the additional ½ cup flour until the dough is firm but elastic. If needed, add in a few more drops of water during the mixing process.

Brush a large bowl with the olive oil, then place the dough in the bowl, turning to coat on all sides. Cover the bowl with a damp dish towel and let rise for 1 hour or until dough doubles in size.

Punch the dough down, and let it rest for 10 more minutes. While resting, line a baking sheet with parchment paper.

Divide the dough into 8 equal pieces. One at a time, gently roll the dough pieces in a circular fashion against a countertop until they form a perfect ball.

Coat a finger in flour and then poke a hole in the middle of the dough ball, slowly stretching the hole to about 1½ inches in diameter. Place the bagels on the parchment paper–lined baking sheet.

Preheat the oven to 425°F. Bring a large pot of water to a boil and add the brown sugar or barley malt syrup, the remaining ½ teaspoon of salt, and the baking soda. Using a slotted spoon or skimmer, add bagels to the water and let them boil for 2 minutes on each side. (You will likely need to do this in batches so you don't overcrowd the bagels.) Place boiled bagels back on the baking sheet. If desired, top the bagels with toppings.

Bake in the oven for 20 minutes or until golden brown. Let cool on a wire rack.

FUN FACT

The cinematography for New York sequences in the film was inspired by the shooting style of 1970s films. The lens package was actually inspired by films from the era like *Manhattan*, *Dog Day Afternoon*, and *Marathon Man* in an effort to achieve the kind of distortion, aberrations, and style filmmakers wanted in those scenes, allowing the focus to be on the characters while the chaotic background falls away.

Soul, 2020

22-STYLE GYRO

Entrée | YIELD: 6 gyros

The spirited soul 22 once got in a fight with Archimedes over the proper pronunciation of an iconic Greek treat. Regardless of who was right (it was Archimedes), everyone can agree on the greatness of this 22-Style Gyro. Ground beef, lamb, and a bevy of vegetables are doused in tzatziki and wrapped in pita bread. With its feta cheese crumbles and just a hint of rosemary, the 22-Style Gyro is a truly inspired creation.

GYRO MEAT:

1 yellow onion, roughly chopped

1 pound 80/20 ground beef

1 pound ground lamb

4 cloves garlic

2 tablespoons dried oregano

1 tablespoon dried thyme

3 teaspoons kosher salt

2 teaspoons freshly ground black pepper

2 teaspoons cumin

1 teaspoon rosemary, chopped fine

½ cup olive oil, divided

TO MAKE THE MEAT:

Preheat the oven to 350°F.

Place the chopped onion into a food processor and process until smooth. Drain any liquid, and then put the puréed onion into a cheesecloth, kitchen cloth, or a couple of paper towels, and squeeze out any additional liquid. Add the onions back into the food processor.

Add the beef, lamb, garlic, oregano, thyme, salt, pepper, cumin, and rosemary into the food processor and pulse a few times until the mixture comes together. Purée for 1 minute or until fully smooth and mixed.

Place the meat mixture into a loaf pan, pressing down on the meat to pack it in as densely as possible.

Cook the meat in the oven for 60 minutes, taking it out halfway to pour out any grease pooling at the top and to turn the loaf pan 90 degrees. At the end of the 60 minutes, the meat should have an internal temperature of 160°F.

TZATZIKI:

1 English cucumber

12 ounces plain Greek yogurt

2 tablespoons olive oil

1 tablespoon lemon juice

1 tablespoon minced garlic

½ teaspoon dill

Salt and pepper, to taste

GYRO TOPPINGS:

6 pieces pita bread

1 cup shredded lettuce

1 Roma tomato, sliced

½ red onion, sliced

½ cup crumbled feta cheese

SPECIAL TOOLS NEEDED:

Food processor

Loaf pan

Meat thermometer

TO MAKE THE TZATZIKI SAUCE:

While the meat cooks, prepare the tzatziki sauce: Peel and deseed the cucumber (cut the cucumber in half, then use a spoon to scoop out the soft, seeded middle of the cucumber). Grate the cucumber into a small bowl and squeeze out any excess liquid. In a medium bowl, combine the grated cucumber, yogurt, olive oil, lemon juice, garlic, and dill. Mix and add salt and pepper to taste. Store in the refrigerator until you are ready for it.

Once the gyro meat is removed from the oven, drain it again and weigh it down by pushing another loaf pan or some cans over aluminum foil on top of it, and let rest for 15 minutes. Cut into very thin slices. Heat 2 tablespoons of olive oil in a large pan over medium-high heat and place meat slices on the pan for 1 minute each side or until browned and slightly crispy. (Do this in batches until you have 24 pieces.)

Prepare 6 gyro sandwiches by spreading 2 tablespoons of tzatziki on each pita, then add lettuce, tomato, onion, and feta to one side. Add 4 gyro meat slices to each pita, and fold over.

FUN FACT

Filmmakers wanted a very specific look to the soul world of The Great Before, including how the grass would look. According to filmmakers, it was not supposed to look like grass but feel like it. The challenge was that Pixar's technology actually allows for each individual blade of grass to be created—which was not the desired look. So technicians had to modify existing technology to give the grass a more painterly look—some individual blades mixed into a larger, softer look.

Soul, 2020

THE SWEET LIFE PECAN PIE

Dessert | YIELD: One 12-inch pie | Vegetarian

As 22 knows, you can't crush a soul in The Great Before—that's what life on Earth is for. But even a Lost Soul would take solace—and perhaps even find its purpose—in this Sweet Life Pecan Pie. Sugar, butter, and plenty of pecans come together in an absolutely delectable dessert. When food is this good, it's bound to inspire greatness. One taste might even help a certain curmudgeonly soul realize that life can actually be pretty sweet.

PIE CRUST:

1¼ cups all-purpose flour, plus more for dusting

½ teaspoon kosher salt

½ tablespoons granulated sugar

½ cup unsalted butter, cold and cut into small cubes

¼ cup cold water

FILLING:

1 cup granulated sugar

1 cup corn syrup

⅓ cup salted butter

1 tablespoon water

2 teaspoons cornstarch

3 eggs

¼ teaspoon kosher salt

1 teaspoon vanilla

1 cup chopped pecans

GARNISH:

30 whole pecans

Whipped cream

Note:
Limited on time? Use a pre-made (pre-cooked) pie crust and skip to step 6.

TO MAKE THE PIE CRUST:

Mix the flour, salt, and sugar together in a large bowl.

Place the butter cubes in the bowl with the flour mixture, and using your hands, squeeze and mix everything together until fully mixed and slightly crumbly.

Slowly add the water as you mix and continue to mix until the dough fully sticks together. If it's still crumbly, add a bit more water.

Form the dough into a ball and then press into a disc. Wrap in plastic wrap and refrigerate for 1 hour.

Flour a large surface and roll the dough out with a rolling pin until it's 12 inches in diameter. Place in a pie pan and press down, crimping the edges.

Preheat the oven to 350°F.

TO MAKE THE FILLING:

Combine the sugar, corn syrup, butter, water, and cornstarch in a medium saucepan over medium heat. Bring to a boil and then remove from heat.

Whisk the eggs in a small bowl and then slowly add into the syrup mixture, stirring constantly. Add the salt, vanilla, and pecans and stir again.

Pour the syrup mixture into the pie pan.

TO MAKE THE GARNISH:

Garnish the top of the pie with additional whole pecans, and then bake in the oven for 45 to 50 minutes. The pie will be firm—if you touch the center, it should spring back slightly.

Move to a wire rack and let cool.

Slice and top each slice with whipped cream.

Soul, 2020

STREETS OF NY PIZZA

Entrée | YIELD: Two 14-inch pizzas (8 slices, cut NY-style)

The streets of the Big Apple are ripe for the culinary picking. From gyros to bagels to the ever-popular cheesecake, the city that never sleeps is chockful of delectable selections. But perhaps the most quintessential meal for any proper New Yorker is a slice of pizza. The spirited soul 22 experiences a life-changing moment when she takes her first bite of this classic New York cuisine. And this interpretation of that much-loved meal is sure to please diners of *all* realms. Smothered in mozzarella and dotted with pepperoni, Streets of NY Pizza is one of life's joys that nobody should miss out on.

PIZZA DOUGH:

3½ cups bread flour, plus more for dusting

1 teaspoon active dry yeast

1 teaspoon granulated sugar

1 teaspoon kosher salt

2 cups lukewarm water

1 tablespoon olive oil, plus more for greasing

SAUCE:

One 28-ounce can of whole peeled tomatoes (San Marzano preferred)

½ tablespoon kosher salt

¼ cup olive oil

TOPPINGS:

12 ounces whole milk low-moisture mozzarella, cut into ½-inch cubes, divided

4 ounces sliced pepperoni, divided

SPECIAL TOOLS NEEDED:

Pizza stone and pizza peel (or large baking sheet)

Cutting board

Pizza cutter, mezzaluna, or large knife

TO MAKE THE PIZZA DOUGH:

Combine the flour, yeast, sugar, and salt in a large bowl.

Add the water and the olive oil, mixing with your hands until fully combined.

Move the dough to a floured surface and knead for 5 minutes, until the dough is smooth and elastic. (Add more flour, 1 tablespoon at a time, if the dough is too sticky.)

Place the dough into an oiled bowl, cover with plastic wrap, and let rise in the fridge overnight.

TO MAKE THE SAUCE:

Pour the can of tomatoes into a bowl and crush the tomatoes with your hands until a chunky sauce forms. Whisk in the salt and olive oil until the olive oil and tomato sauce are fully emulsified. Refrigerate until you're ready to use. (You'll have some sauce left over after this recipe.)

TO MAKE THE PIZZA:

Remove the dough from the fridge and cut the dough in half—we'll be making two pizzas.

Place a pizza stone in the oven and preheat the oven as high as it will go (most likely 500° to 550°F). Preheat with the stone in the oven for 1 hour. Don't have a stone? Place a baking sheet in the oven while it preheats.

Take one dough ball and place onto a floured surface. With floured hands, slowly stretch the disc into a large circle by holding one edge and continuing to rotate along the edge, letting gravity stretch it downwards. Continue until the pizza crust is 12 to 14 inches in diameter and even in thickness.

Place the pizza crust onto a pizza peel (or the preheated baking sheet, sprayed with oil).

Place ¾ cup of sauce in the middle of the pizza crust and use the back of a spoon to lightly spread it around the rest of the crust, leaving a ½-inch border around the edge. Sprinkle half of the cheese evenly on top of the sauce, then top with half of the pepperoni.

Transfer the pizza onto the pizza stone (or place on the preheated baking sheet and into the oven) and bake for 12 to 15 minutes, or until the crust is brown and the cheese is melted and beginning to brown.

Remove the pizza from the oven and transfer onto a cutting board. Let sit for a few minutes and cut into 4 large pieces.

To make the second pizza, repeat steps 8 through 12.

FUN FACT

Pixar's efforts to create authentic worlds got a little sticky when it came to the New York City sequences. Filmmakers who visited the city on research trips noticed a lot of black spots on the ground in the city—the source? Chewing gum that's been walked on by millions of New Yorkers. Those spots found their way into the film's sets.

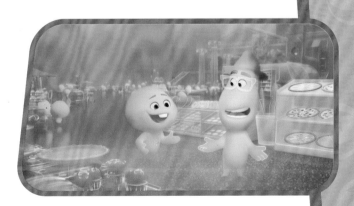

MOVIE SPOTLIGHT:
LUCA

Memorable Quote: "Silenzio, Bruno!"

Release Year: 2021

Director: Enrico Casarosa

Pixar's twenty-fourth feature film is a beautiful, coming-of-age adventure set amidst the backdrop of the Italian coast. Sea monster Luca has always been curious about the world above the ocean. Although his parents attempt to instill a solid sense of fear in their ever-cautious son, Luca and his newfound sea monster friend Alberto eventually find their way to the surface . . . and discover a world of adventure unlike anything they've ever seen. Luca and Alberto meet a spunky human girl named Giulia, and together they form a team to compete in a triathlon called the Portorosso Cup. And Luca does it all with a growing appreciation for the extraordinary cuisine that Italy has to offer. Luca quickly discovers that with good friends—and good food!—by his side, he can do anything . . . and have the best summer ever in the process.

Luca director Enrico Casarosa based his inspiring film on his childhood adventures along the Italian Riviera. Together with his thrill-seeking best friend, Alberto (the namesake of *Luca's* Alberto!), Enrico explored the narrow roads of his hometown of Genoa, took trains to the beaches that line the Italian coast, and leapt from harrowing cliffs into the refreshing Ligurian Sea. And just like Luca, Casarosa shared countless meals with his own Alberto—from focaccia to *farinata* (Ligurian flatbread), gelato, and *ghiaccioli* (ice pops!).

When crafting *Luca,* Casarosa centered many of his characters' key moments around the foods he remembered from his childhood. Luca, Alberto, and Giulia swap stories while enjoying slices of *anguria* (watermelon) and decadent cones of gelato. And Luca and Alberto learn the meaning of acceptance when Giulia's dad, Massimo, welcomes them to his home with his signature dish—*trenette al pesto.* Casarosa based Massimo's home-cooked meal on his own family's recipe . . . then graciously shared it with the world so everyone could enjoy a taste of his hometown! (Find it on page 181 of this book!)

When preparing to animate *Luca,* Pixar's filmmakers traveled to the Italian Riviera. There, they observed the culture and architecture of this fabled location and enjoyed sweet and savory meals in the name of research. They even got to enjoy a dinner at the Genoa home of Casarosa's parents! And in animating *Luca,* filmmakers were sure to include a nod to another beloved Pixar film. The Pizza Planet truck makes a cameo on the streets of Portorosso . . . as a three-wheeled Italian vehicle!

With fun, friendship, and food at its always-welcoming heart, *Luca* shows the world that underdogs can do anything so long as they stick together, that Brunos can indeed be silenced, and that sometimes you just have to take a great big leap. But perhaps *Luca's* most poignant message comes from Giulia, who once said, "There may be a million things you think you can't do. All you need is a chance to try." It's a lesson that applies to life, as well as to the vast variety of foods that *Luca* serves up. *Buon appetito!*

ERCOLE'S FOCACCIA SANDWICH

Entrée | YIELD: 1 very large sandwich (6 to 8 servings)

Portorosso's resident bully loves eating his sandwiches. And while Ercole's personality leaves a lot to be desired, his go-to meal is a proper Portorosso favorite. Ercole's Focaccia Sandwich piles mortadella, provolone, and tomato between two generous slices of homemade focaccia. It's a culinary masterpiece that's perfect for sharing with true friends. And as for Ercole, he isn't nearly as intimidating as he seems . . . at least, not after he takes a bite of this truly epic sandwich!

1 package active dry yeast (2¼ teaspoons)

1 tablespoon granulated sugar

1½ cups lukewarm water

4 cups all-purpose flour, plus additional for dusting

¼ cup olive oil, plus 2 tablespoons for topping, and additional for greasing

1 tablespoon kosher salt

¾ tablespoon flake salt, for topping

¼ cup Dijon mustard

½ pound mortadella, sliced

½ pound provolone, sliced

1 tomato, sliced

SPECIAL TOOLS NEEDED:

Mixer

Rolling pin

Basting brush

Combine the yeast, sugar, and lukewarm water in a large mixing bowl. Let stand 10 minutes or until foamy.

Add the flour, olive oil, and kosher salt to the bowl. Mix with a dough hook attachment, slowly at first, and then on medium speed once the flour is incorporated. Mix for 5 minutes or until it forms a sticky dough. If you don't have a mixer, mix the dough together by hand, and then knead it on a floured surface for 5 minutes.

Move the dough into a large oiled bowl and cover with a damp towel. Let sit in a warm location for 1 hour, or until the dough has doubled in size.

Transfer the dough to a floured surface and use a floured rolling pin or your hands to shape into a 4-by-24-inch rectangle approximately ½ inch thick. Cover the dough with a damp towel and let rise for 20 minutes.

While waiting for it to rise, preheat the oven to 400°F.

Transfer the dough to a greased baking sheet and poke deep indents into the bread with your finger (all the way to the bottom without creating a hole). Brush olive oil along the surface of the bread, allowing it to pool in the indents. Sprinkle with flake salt.

Bake the bread for 20 minutes, or until dough is evenly golden. (Remove the bread from the oven and give a tap on the bottom of the loaf to test doneness—if it sounds hollow, it's done!)

Let cool, then slice in half widthwise. Spread the mustard on the bottom, then top with a layer of mortadella, a layer of provolone, and tomato slices. Cover with the top slice.

Find someone to watch you eat the big sandwich (or cut it into 6 to 8 smaller sandwiches, if you want to share).

FUN FACT

All of the background kid voices in the film were recorded by local children in Italy.

Luca, 2021

PORTOROSSO CUP PASTA

Entrée | YIELD: 4 bowls of pasta | Vegetarian

Residents of the charming town of Portorosso take great pride in their annual competition, the Portorosso Cup. This race challenges young entrants to swim, cycle, and of course, eat lots and lots of pasta. Inspired by this most unusual event, Portorosso Cup Pasta combines three different shapes of pasta in a delightfully seasoned dish, topping it off with a trio of sauces to represent the colors of the Italian flag. This quintessential meal is packed with both flavor and carbohydrates, making it the perfect dish to enjoy while training for a highly competitive race!

Pesto Sauce (from the Trenette al Pesto recipe, page 181)

ALFREDO SAUCE:

¼ cup salted butter

1 cup heavy cream

1 cup Parmesan cheese

¼ teaspoon garlic powder

¼ teaspoon kosher salt

⅛ teaspoon freshly ground black pepper

TOMATO SAUCE:

1 tablespoon olive oil

2 cloves garlic, minced

8 ounces canned crushed tomatoes

1 tablespoon water

¼ teaspoon granulated sugar

¼ teaspoon oregano

Dash of kosher salt

Dash of freshly ground black pepper

Dash of red pepper flakes

10 leaves fresh basil, chopped

TO MAKE THE PESTO SAUCE:

Make the pesto sauce according to the directions in the Trenette al Pesto recipe. You will only use half for this recipe. Set aside.

TO MAKE THE ALFREDO SAUCE:

Melt the butter in a large saucepan over low heat, then add the cream. Cook until the cream begins to bubble, about 5 minutes. Remove from heat and whisk in the Parmesan, garlic, salt, and pepper until melted and smooth.

TO MAKE THE TOMATO SAUCE:

Heat the olive oil in a seperate large saucepan over medium heat and add the garlic. Sauté for 1 minute or until fragrant, then add the tomatoes, water, sugar, oregano, salt, black pepper, and red pepper flakes. Bring to a boil over medium-high heat and then reduce to low and simmer for 8 to 10 minutes or until sauce is reduced. Turn off the heat, add freshly chopped basil and salt to taste. Set aside.

PASTA:

1 teaspoon kosher salt

6 ounces spaghetti

6 ounces rotini

6 ounces farfalle

SPECIAL TOOLS NEEDED:

Food processor

TO MAKE THE PASTA:

Add the salt to a large pot of water and bring to a boil over medium-high heat. Add in the pastas and cook according to their packages' directions. (Cooking time may vary based on the shape—you can cook these separately, if so.)

Drain pasta. If not already mixed together, mix the shapes together and divide between four bowls.

Top each bowl with a vertical stripe of pesto sauce on the left, a vertical stripe of alfredo sauce in the middle, and a vertical stripe of tomato sauce on the right.

Serve and see how quickly you can finish a bowl!

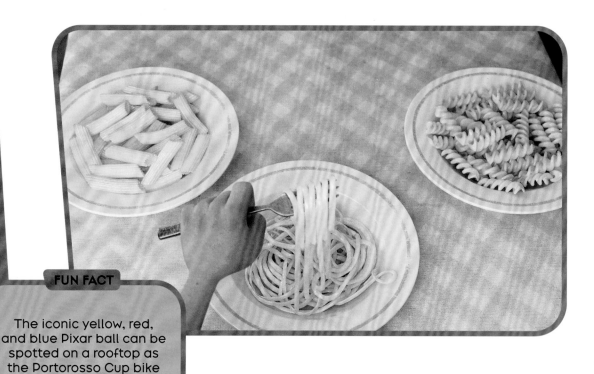

FUN FACT

The iconic yellow, red, and blue Pixar ball can be spotted on a rooftop as the Portorosso Cup bike race gets underway.

Luca, 2021

PORTOROSSO GELATO

Dessert | YIELD: 5 cups of gelato | Vegetarian, Gluten Free

In Portorosso, sea monsters have avoided humans for as long as anyone can remember. After all, it's easy to fear what you don't understand. But some things are universal—like friendship, family, and of course, the love of gelato! Portorosso Gelato is a fun twist on the classic *stracciatella*—its blue, green, and purple candy melts mimic the colors of the town's much-feared sea monsters. It's an adorably delicious dessert that's bound to be a hit with any resident of Portorosso—including those who aren't usually so accepting of people (and sea monsters) who are different. After all, if there's one thing that's bound to bring everyone together, it's gelato. *È spettacolare!*

2 cups whole milk

1 cup heavy cream

1 cup granulated sugar

1 teaspoon vanilla extract

3 tablespoons each blue, green, and purple candy melts

SPECIAL TOOLS NEEDED:

Ice cream maker
(optional)

Pour the milk, cream, and sugar into a large saucepan and cook over low heat, mixing often, for 5 minutes or until sugar has dissolved. Do not allow the contents to boil! Stir in the vanilla.

Transfer the contents to a heat-safe bowl, cover, and refrigerate for 30 minutes or until slightly cooled.

Transfer to an ice cream maker and follow manufacturer's instructions to finish making the gelato. Don't have an ice cream maker? Transfer the contents into a freezer-safe container and place in the freezer for 5 hours, taking it out, breaking the surface, and mixing every 30 minutes until fully frozen.

Once the gelato is beginning to freeze, melt the candy melts in separate bowls in a microwave, stirring every 30 seconds.

Pour the melted candy onto the top of the gelato while it's halfway through freezing (2½ hours if freezing/mixing by hand, and halfway through the instructions if using an ice cream maker). The candy will harden on contact—stir up the gelato to break the candy into small pieces, even smaller than chocolate chips.

Continue freezing until gelato is completed. If hard, let sit at room temperature for 5 minutes to soften, then serve.

FUN FACT

There is a poster for Walt Disney's *20,000 Leagues Under the Sea*, which opened in December 1954, at the cinema in Portorosso.

Luca, 2021

TRENETTE AL PESTO

Entrée | YIELD: 4 servings | Vegetarian

The Vespa may well be the greatest thing ever created, but pasta is a very close second! And in Italy, cherished pasta recipes are passed from parent to child, and friend to friend. Giulia's papa, Massimo, was lucky enough to receive this tried-and-true recipe from his very good friend—*Luca* director Enrico Casarosa. Fresh basil, garlic, and olive oil come together in a homemade pesto, while potatoes, green beans, and pasta are boiled to perfection. Topped with pine nuts and cheese, and tossed with oil, Trenette al Pesto offers a fusion of flavors that truly is *perfetto*. This beloved Marcovaldo (and Casarosa!) family dish is destined to become a hit with families, friends, and underdogs alike. *Buon appetito*!

45 fresh basil leaves (about 1 packed cup)

2 cloves garlic

Pinch of coarse salt

½ cup (100 ml) extra-virgin olive oil, divided

1 handful (about ¼ cup) pine nuts

2 tablespoons grated parmigiano cheese

2 tablespoons grated pecorino cheese

16 ounces trenette pasta (or any pasta you love: linguini, spaghetti, etc.)

1 cup green beans, cut in 1-inch pieces

1 large yellow potato, cut in 1-inch cubes

SPECIAL TOOLS NEEDED:

Mortar and pestle or food processor

Let's start with the pesto: Put the basil and the garlic in a marble mortar with a pinch of coarse salt and start mashing with the pestle. Slowly add a bit of oil as you go. If you don't have a mortar and pestle, a food processor will work too. In fact, that's what most people use in Liguria nowadays!

Next, add the pine nuts, the grated parmigiano, and the grated pecorino. As you continue to add the olive oil, the consistency should be that of a very dense cream, and the quantity of oil needed will vary depending on the mixture's degree of absorption. The key for a great-tasting pesto is to not cook your basil. If you use a food processor, don't let it run too long or it will heat the ingredients.

At this point, you can boil the water for the pasta. Once it boils, add some coarse salt to the pot. Throw in the pasta as well as the green beans and the potato. Drain the pasta once it's cooked but still "al dente"—not too soft! (Use the recommended time on your pasta's packaging.) Save a little bit of the pasta water for the sauce.

Place the pesto on the bottom of the serving bowl, add a couple of spoonfuls of the pasta water, then add the pasta to the bowl with the pesto. Mix it well, then serve it!

FUN FACT

Keep an eye out for the Pizza Planet truck in the form of a Piaggio Ape parked on a street in Portorosso.

Luca, 2021

WATERMELON SPLASH

Drink | YIELD: 4 servings | Vegetarian, Vegan, Dairy Free, Gluten Free

For Luca, Alberto, and Giulia, a chilled slice of watermelon is the perfect way to cool off on a hot day in Portorosso. It's the quintessential summer snack that's ideal for sharing with a group of fellow underdogs. This Watermelon Splash offers a flavorful twist on the trio's go-to snack. Blended watermelon, mint, and lime come together to create an icy spritzer that evokes fond memories of summertime at the seaside on the Italian coast.

1 small watermelon (about 5 pounds)

8 to 10 mint leaves

Ice cubes

1 large lime, juiced, divided

16 ounces sparkling water

1 lime, cut into wedges, for garnish

SPECIAL TOOLS NEEDED:

Blender

Sieve

Muddler

Shaker

Cut the watermelon into cubes and place in a blender. Blend until puréed and pulpy.

Strain through a sieve into a large bowl, saving all of the liquid and discarding the pulp. (The watermelon should create around 24 ounces of juice.) Set aside.

Muddle half the mint leaves in the bottom of a shaker. Add a handful of ice cubes, half of the watermelon juice, and the juice from half of a lime. Cover and shake until the outside of the shaker is frosty.

Prep two glasses with a handful of ice cubes and strain the mixture between the two. Top off with sparkling water and a wedge of lime for garnish.

Repeat steps 3 and 4 for the other two glasses.

FUN FACT

Jack Dylan Grazer (voice of Alberto) recorded every single line of dialogue inside his mother's closet.

MOVIE SPOTLIGHT:
TURNING RED

Memorable Quote: "We've all got an inner beast."

Release Year: 2022

Director: Domee Shi

Thirteen-year-old Meilin Lee is a perfectly ordinary Chinese-Canadian girl. She's a dutiful daughter, a hardworking student, and along with her friends, a devoted fan of the much-loved boyband 4*Town. But when Mei learns that the women in her family have the power to turn into giant red pandas—and worse, that she's inherited this so-called "gift" herself—her overly structured life begins to crumble. She's forced to live a double life—one in which she never knows exactly when she might turn red. But although Mei's inner panda definitely makes things more complicated, it ultimately forces Mei's mother, Ming, to accept her for who she truly is . . . and shows Mei that when things get hard, her friends and her family will always come to her aid. As Ming says, "Don't hold back for anyone. The farther you go, the prouder I'll be." And Mei *and* her red panda are ready to go the distance.

Like many Pixar films, *Turning Red* includes scenes set in the kitchen and around the table. But it also utilizes food as a tool through which to show the characters' ever-changing relationships. Mei's father, Jin, takes his time in crafting a delectable pork belly stir fry, which he presents to his wife and daughter—a culinary way to show his emotional affection. Ming prepares a smiling breakfast congee for Mei—a not-so-subtle reminder that her Mei-Mei is meant to behave as the perfect, cheerful child. And Mei's extended family gathers over a large meal, where they share stories of encouragement (along with a few matriarchal admonitions) to help Mei prepare to banish her inner panda forever. Flavored with rich spices and spiked with the occasional hidden agenda, the food in *Turning Red* is as complex as the characters themselves. As Mei explains, "We've all got an inner beast. We've all got a messy, loud, weird part of ourselves hidden away. And a lot of us never let it out. But I did. How about you?"

TURNING RED BEAN PASTE BAO

Appetizer | YIELD: 36 bao | Vegetarian, Vegan, Dairy Free

Comfort food is universal. It soothes the soul, quiets the mind, and serves as a tasty reminder that no matter how stressful any given moment may be, one can always find solace in a tried-and-true recipe. For Meilin Lee, that comfort comes from bao. It helps to keep Mei grounded as she learns to control her often overwhelming shifts into the red panda and reminds her that even when everything seems to be changing, some things can remain blissfully the same. *Turning Red* Bean Paste Bao is the perfect comfort food for those moments when life feels just a little too wild—whether that feeling comes from school, work, or a particularly unpredictable inner red panda.

4 cups all-purpose flour, plus more for dusting

1½ tablespoons granulated sugar

¾ teaspoon active dry yeast

2 cups water

16 ounces red bean paste

SPECIAL TOOLS NEEDED:

Steamer basket

FUN FACT

Filmmakers placed the Pizza Planet truck in Chinatown with a custom Chinese version of the Pizza Planet logo (as if it's from a Chinatown franchise of the Pizza Planet chain).

Mix the flour, sugar, and yeast in a large mixing bowl.

Add the water and knead until a solid dough ball forms. If it gets too sticky, add more flour, 1 tablespoon at a time. If it's too dry, add more water, 1 tablespoon at a time.

Cover the bowl with plastic wrap and let the dough rise for 2 hours.

Once your dough has risen, dust your countertop with flour and roll out the dough into a long rope, using the "windmill technique." (Poke a hole through the middle of the dough, and start rotating the dough, holding onto the edges, allowing the dough to stretch out into a long rope circle. Cut one side to form a large dough rope.)

Cut the dough rope into ½-inch pieces. Roll each piece out into a circle to be used as the bao wrapper (about 3 inches in diameter).

Spoon ½ tablespoon red bean paste into the center of each wrapper. Then carefully pinch and fold the wrapper closed, twisting the top to finish. Make sure to press the dough tight to seal the top.

Bring a pot of water to a boil over high heat. Place the baos in a steamer basket lined with parchment paper to prevent sticking and place the basket on top of the boiling pot of water. Close the lid. Steam for 15 minutes, then turn off heat and let the baos rest for 5 minutes.

Turning Red, 2022

JIN'S STIR FRY

Entrée | YIELD: 4 servings | Dairy Free

The women in Meilin Lee's family harbor a secret power—they have the ability to turn into giant red pandas! But Mei's father also has a special gift. Jin is a talented cook—one who shows his love for his family through carefully cultivated cuisine. Stir fry is one of his specialties, and this Jin-inspired dish is nearly as jaw-dropping as Mei's ability to change forms. Pork, lettuce, and an array of spices all blend together in this savory dish. Jin's Stir Fry is the perfect meal to serve at a family gathering . . . or after a particularly raucous boy band concert. Pandas unite!

2 tablespoons soy sauce

½ tablespoon sesame oil

1 teaspoon oyster sauce

½ teaspoon granulated sugar

½ teaspoon kosher salt

½ head iceberg lettuce

2 tablespoons canola oil, divided

1 pound pork belly, skin removed and sliced

1 slice fresh ginger

4 cloves garlic, sliced

2 red chile peppers, sliced thin

3 green onions, sliced thin and green and white parts separated

In a small bowl, combine the soy sauce, sesame oil, oyster sauce, sugar, and salt. Set aside.

Rinse and dry the lettuce and cut or tear into large pieces. Set aside.

Heat a wok over medium-high heat and add ½ tablespoon oil and the pork belly. Cook the pork belly for 2 minutes or until browned. Move to the side of the wok.

Add the remaining 1½ tablespoons oil, the ginger, garlic, chile peppers, and the white part of the green onions into the wok. Cook for 30 seconds or until fragrant.

Turn the heat up to high and add the lettuce, cooking while stirring for 30 seconds.

Add the sauce and stir together, coating the pork and lettuce. Cook for 1 minute, or until lettuce is seared but still crunchy. Top with sliced green onions.

SPECIAL TOOLS NEEDED:

Wok

FUN FACT

The number from several Pixar veterans' CalArts classroom, A113, can be seen on the chalk machine that Jin Lee operates near the end of the movie.

Turning Red, 2022

SMILING CONGEE

Entrée | YIELD: 4 servings of congee | Dairy Free

The Lees place a lot of value on their traditions. This Chinese-Canadian family runs one of the oldest temples in Toronto, and they use the site for worship, education, and to honor their unique cultural heritage. But everyday traditions make their way into Mei's life, too: She starts each morning with a warm bowl of congee. This popular dish offers a healthy, protein-packed start to a hard day at middle school—or working at the family temple. Flavored with ginger and topped with eggs and a soy sauce smile, Smiling Congee is sure to earn a grin . . . or inspire a spontaneous cartwheel.

1 cup jasmine rice, uncooked

8 cups chicken broth

1-inch knob ginger, peeled and sliced thin

½ teaspoon kosher salt

2 tablespoons canola oil

8 eggs

2 stalks green onion

1 cremini mushroom

Soy sauce, for garnish

Rinse the rice until the water drains clear.

Place the rice, chicken broth, ginger, and salt in a large pot and bring to a boil. Once boiling, reduce heat to low and let simmer for 1 hour, or until the mixture is smooth, thick, and creamy.

When the congee is almost done, prepare the toppings. Place the canola oil in a large nonstick pan over medium heat and crack the eggs into the pan. Cover the pan and cook for 2 to 3 minutes or until the whites are set. Then, cut the green onions into eight 1½-inch chunks, dice the rest, and slice the mushroom into 4 slices.

Place the congee in four separate bowls, topping with 2 eggs for eyes, 2 long green onions for eyebrows, diced green onions for hair, a mushroom slice for the nose, and a splash of soy sauce for the mouth.

FUN FACT

The chess move Mei plays with Mr. Gao was inspired by an established chess opening sequence called the "Queen's Gambit."

Lightyear, 2022

SPICY VINES

Side | YIELD: 1 pound asparagus | Vegetarian, Vegan, Dairy Free, Gluten Free

The vegetation on T'Kani Prime is fierce. While greenery on other planets may inspire feelings of peace and serenity, the plants of T'Kani Prime have been known to instill a fair amount of fear. After all, these particular vines just happen to be carnivorous . . . and they're prone to attack unsuspecting passersby. Like those pernicious plants, these *Lightyear*-inspired Spicy Vines will grab hold of their diners—but for all the right reasons. Lightly sautéed and perfectly seasoned, Spicy Vines—like their namesake—are a little bit feisty . . . and that's definitely a good thing!

2 tablespoons olive oil, divided

4 cloves garlic, minced

1 pound fresh asparagus, trimmed

Pinch of kosher salt and freshly ground black pepper, plus more to taste

1 tablespoon chili crisp

2 tablespoons ground salted peanuts

Heat 1 tablespoon of olive oil in a large wok or pan over high heat.

Add the garlic and cook for 1 minute, or until fragrant and crisp. Remove and put in a small bowl, then set aside.

Add another tablespoon of olive oil to your pan or wok, then add the asparagus and salt and pepper. Sauté for 5 to 7 minutes or until crisp-tender.

Mix the chili crisp with the crisp garlic and add to the pan. Mix.

Top the asparagus with the ground peanuts and serve.

FUN FACT

In *Lightyear*, Buzz Lightyear notes the spongy terrain as he explores his unfamiliar surroundings. It's a direct callback to *Toy Story* when Buzz Lightyear first appears on-screen, bounces on Andy's bed, and reports in his mission log that the "terrain seems a bit unstable."

Lightyear, 2022

MEAT-BREAD-MEAT SANDWICH

Entrée | YIELD: 1 sandwich

When Space Ranger Buzz Lightyear finds himself stranded in the future, he quickly discovers that everything has changed. From the planet to his friends to the very concept of food itself, nothing is as he left it. The Meat-Bread-Meat Sandwich offers a playful nod to one of Buzz's more confusing encounters. With two layers of meat on the outside, and bread and vegetables in the middle, this highly unusual sandwich is best eaten in the company of a personal companion robot who can offer a napkin—or several! It's an unexpectedly amusing dish that's absolutely out of this world!

2 tablespoons mayonnaise

¼ teaspoon sriracha

1 piece white bread

½ cucumber, sliced in rounds

2 pieces deli ham, sliced thick

In a small bowl, combine the mayonnaise and sriracha to create a spicy mayo.

Spread the mayo on both sides of the bread.

Cut the cucumber into rounds ¼ inch thick.

On a plate, layer one piece of ham, then 4 cucumber slices, then the bread, then another 4 cucumber slices, and the final piece of ham.

Enjoy your moist sandwich and your juicy fingers.

Note:
Making this sandwich fresh instead of from a vending machine? Add in a slice of Swiss cheese, some lettuce, and a slice of tomato to make it even more delicious.

FUN FACT

Months into production, filmmakers set a lofty goal: *Lightyear* would be Pixar's first feature film made specifically for IMAX screens. After a research trip to IMAX headquarters in Los Angeles, the team created Pixar's first IMAX pipeline for film production, enabling them to simultaneously shoot for IMAX and crop down for standard 2.39:1 format. As a result, audiences experience approximately 30 minutes of thrilling, action-packed IMAX scenes within *Lightyear*.

Elemental, 2023

EMBER'S LOLLIPOPS

Dessert | YIELD: About 20 lollipops | Vegetarian, Vegan, Dairy Free, Gluten Free

Ember is a girl of many talents. But perhaps her sweetest gift is her ability to melt down and sculpt lollipops into a wide array of shapes. While candy art may seem a complicated endeavor, Ember proves that with a spark of determination, anything is possible. These lollipops combine corn syrup, sugar, and water with an array of flavors to create unique candy forms that will truly ignite your taste buds.

2 cups granulated sugar

⅔ cup light corn syrup

¼ cup water

2 teaspoons clear flavor extract (vanilla, mint, etc.) (optional)

SPECIAL TOOLS NEEDED:

Candy thermometer

Lollipop sticks

Pastry brush

Line a large baking sheet with parchment paper or a silicone baking mat. Set aside.

Place the sugar, corn syrup, and water in a medium heavy-bottomed pot over medium-high heat. Bring the mix to a boil, stirring until the sugar has dissolved. Use a wet pastry brush to brush down the sides of the pan to prevent any crystals from forming.

Allow the mixture to boil for 5 to 7 minutes or until the temperature reaches 300°F.

Remove the mixture from the heat and allow to cool until the mixture has stopped boiling. Mix in any optional flavor extracts.

Using a spoon, pour the hot mixture onto the parchment paper or silicone mat, making fun shapes. Place lollipop sticks in the center of the pops and pour a small additional amount of the mixture on top of the spot where the stick meets the lollipop, to fully enclose it.

Let cool and harden for about 10 minutes.

Elemental, 2023

KOL-NUTS

Dessert | YIELD: 32 truffles | Vegetarian, Gluten Free

Ember and Wade couldn't be more different. One exudes fiery determination, while the other is the literal embodiment of going with the flow. But one thing they can both agree on is the culinary perfection of kol-nuts. These hazelnut truffles are coated in black cocoa powder, evoking the fiery ambiance of Ember's family store. Made from heavy whipping cream and semisweet chocolate chips, kol-nuts are perfect for sharing with a new friend. After all . . . opposites react.

¾ cup heavy whipping cream

12 ounces semisweet chocolate chips

½ cup unsalted butter

24 hazelnuts

¼ cup black cocoa powder

In a medium saucepan over medium-low heat, heat the cream until simmering.

Turn off the stove and add the chocolate chips into the saucepan. Stir until the chocolate is melted and smooth. Add the butter in small chunks, stirring until fully melted and incorporated.

Pour the chocolate mixture onto a wax paper-lined pie plate or shallow casserole dish. Place in the fridge to chill for 1 hour or until firm but scoopable.

Remove the plate from the fridge and scoop out an overflowing teaspoon of truffle filling. Take a hazelnut and cover with the truffle filling, rolling into a ball, and place on a wax paper-covered plate. Repeat with the rest of the mixture.

Place the black cocoa powder on a plate, then roll the truffles in it, shaking off any excess cocoa.

Elemental, 2023

THE FIREPLACE'S LAVA JAVA

Drink | YIELD: 1 serving | Vegetarian, Vegan, Dairy Free, Gluten Free

Ember knows a thing or two about heat. As a Fire Element, she adores everything hot—from spicy foods to radiant art. And nothing speaks to Ember more than the Fireplace's Lava Java. This coffee with a delightful cinnamon syrup is a perfect morning treat that practically erupts with flavor.

2 tablespoons brown sugar

1 tablespoon water

½ tablespoon granulated sugar

1 teaspoon cinnamon

½ teaspoon vanilla

1 cup dark roasted coffee, ground

Make the cinnamon syrup by placing the brown sugar, water, granulated sugar, cinnamon, and vanilla in a small saucepan over medium-high heat. Heat until simmering, stirring often, then reduce heat to low and cook until sugars have dissolved and a syrup consistency takes form.

Make coffee using your preferred method.

Mix in the syrup and serve hot.

Elemental, 2023

WADE WATER

Drink | **YIELD:** 1 drink | Vegetarian, Vegan, Dairy Free, Gluten Free

Wade Ripple is a go-with-the-flow guy. Nothing ever really phases him—which makes sense, given his highly adaptable nature. He's often seen with a smile on his face, and his go-to pink drink in his hand. Wade Water combines coconut water, green tea, and raspberry syrup in a refreshing beverage full of electrolytes that's sure to quench anyone's thirst.

2 cups coconut water

1 green tea sachet

Ice cubes

1 ounce raspberry syrup

1 lemon wedge

⅛ teaspoon salt

Heat the coconut water and place the green tea sachet in the water, steeping for 3 minutes.

Place the green tea/coconut water in a shaker with ice.

Add the raspberry syrup, juice from 1 lemon wedge, and the salt.

Shake until chilled and pour into a large glass.

SPECIAL TOOLS NEEDED:

Shaker

CONCLUSION

Hey, howdy, hey! We're so glad you've joined us on this one-of-a-kind culinary journey. We've visited lands big and small, with recipes worthy of the tiniest bugs and scariest monsters. We've traveled the world, exploring life in the Great Barrier Reef and the desert pit stop of Radiator Springs. And with dishes that range from the familiar to the almost unimaginable, we've tasted an extraordinary sample of all the things our world—and those that border The Great Beyond—has to offer.

Whether you're an accomplished chef or just learning your way around the kitchen, we hope you've enjoyed this epicurean adventure through some of Pixar's most iconic films. And we hope you'll continue to come back to these recipes with the enthusiasm of a young Super coming into their (many!) powers, the determination of a monster studying the Refined Scare Technique, and the bravery of a Scottish princess shooting for her own hand. The famed chef Auguste Gusteau once pointed out, "Anyone can cook. But only the fearless can be great." And as Pixar has long taught us, the importance of holding on to that hope, determination, and willingness to work hard is a lesson that extends far beyond the kitchen. In fact, its boundaries are limitless—just like our imaginations.

Now, bound, bound, bound, and rebound. To infinity . . . and beyond!

SUGGESTED MENUS

Pixar Picnic

Enjoy a light and delicious meal out in the sun. These recipes are perfect for sharing on a picnic blanket!

- Ancient Grains and Corn Salad (page 133)
- *La Luna* Pies (page 113)
- 5-Second-Rule Grapes (page 124)
- Be My Pal Cupcakes (page 121)

Adventure Pack

Prepare yourself for adventure by packing a backpack full of these sweet and savory snacks and extra-hydrating water.

- *For the Birds* Seed (page 44)
- Kreature Krisps (page 45)
- Ercole's Focaccia Sandwich (page 175)
- Wade Water (page 201)

Brunch

Start your morning off right with this hearty meal and multiple options for drinks—depending on how caffeinated you want to be!

- Sludge Coffee (page 53)
- Homemade Organic Fuel (page 67)
- Breakfast of Supers (page 151)
- Soulful Bagels (page 164)

Tea Party

Enjoy this sweet spread with your favorite tea. Prefer coffee or cocoa? We have recipes for that!

- Berry Board (page 135)
- Jelly Bean Burgers (page 107)
- Heimlich's Boysenberry Pies (page 40)
- Dory's Purple Shells (page 137)
- Ka-Chow Coffee (page 65)
- Parapluie Café Cocoa (page 119)

Diner Dinner

Create a classic diner experience in your own home with these recipes!

- Supernova Burgers (page 31)
- Mine, Mine, Mine Chips (page 58)
- Ellie's Adventure (page 101)
- The Sweet Life Pecan Pie (page 169)

RECIPES ORGANIZED BY TYPE

DIETARY CONSIDERATIONS

───────── ★ ─────────

V: Vegetarian | DF: Dairy Free | GF: Gluten Free | V+: Vegan

CHAPTER ONE:
1984–1999

Bee Stings: V

Luxo Jr. Ball Slice and Bake Cookies: V

Shredded Coconut Snowball Cookies: V

Pizza Planet Pizza: V

Howdy Hot Dogs: DF

Supernova Burgers

Alien Slime Soda: V, V+, DF, GF

Chessboard Cookies: V

Buggy Platter: V

Heimlich's Boysenberry Pies: V

CHAPTER TWO:
2000–2009

For the Birds Seed: V, DF, GF

Kreature Krisps: V

Scream Factory Hot Wings: GF

Harryhausen's Sushi

Abominable Snow Cones: V, V+, DF, GF

Sludge Coffee: V, V+, GF

Nothing Fishy Vegetarian Sushi Rolls: V

"Made Me Ink" Pasta: V

Mine, Mine, Mine Chips: DF, GF

Boundin' Popcorn: V, GF

Frozone Slushie: V, V+, DF, GF

Luigi's Tower of Tires Pasta Salad: V

Ka-Chow Coffee: V, V+, DF, GF

Homemade Organic Fuel: V, V+, DF, GF

Remy's "Lightning-y" Mushrooms: V, GF

Gusteau's Soup: V, GF

Rat-atouille: V, V+, DF, GF

Magnifique Layer Cake: V

Remy's Flight of Flavor: V

Anyone Can Cook Soufflé: V

Presto Carrots: V, GF

Never-Expired Cake: V

Axiom Cupcake in a Cup: V

The Cloudy Concoction: V, V+, DF, GF

Spirit of Adventure Special: GF

Balloon Bouquet Cake Pops: V

Adventure's End Sundae: V, GF

Ellie's Adventure: V, V+, DF, GF

CHAPTER THREE:
2010–2019

Sunrise/Sunset: V, V+, DF, GF

Jelly Bean Burgers: V

Lemon Cookies: V, DF

La Luna Pies: V

Witch's Cakes: V

King's Feast Turkey Legs: DF, GF

Parapluie Café Cocoa: V, GF

Be My Pal Cupcakes: V

I Lava You Cake: V

5-Second-Rule Grapes: V, V+, DF, GF

Candy Tears: V, V+, DF, GF

Broccoli Pizza: V, GF

Brain Freeze: V, V+, DF, GF

Ancient Grains and Corn Salad: V, GF

Berry Board: V

Dory's Purple Shells: V

Pan de Muerto: V

Abuelita's Tamales: DF, GF

Bonding Through Bao: DF

Breakfast of Supers: V

Jack-Jack's Cookie Num-Num: V

The Happy Platter Surprise

CHAPTER FOUR:
2020–TODAY

The Manticore's Tavern Soup of the Day: DF

Burger Shire Second Breakfast Sandwich

Barley's Favorite Cheese Puffs: V

The Manticore's Tavern Roast Beast: DF, GF

Soulful Bagels: V, V+, DF

22-Style Gyro

The Sweet Life Pecan Pie: V

Streets of NY Pizza

Ercole's Focaccia Sandwich

Portorosso Cup Pasta: V

Portorosso Gelato: V, GF

Trenette al Pesto: V

Watermelon Splash: V, V+, DF, GF

Turning Red Bean Paste Bao: V, V+, DF

Jin's Stir Fry: DF

Smiling Congee: DF

Spicy Vines: V, V+, DF, GF

Meat-Bread-Meat Sandwiches

Ember's Lollipops: V, V+, DF, GF

Kol-Nuts: V, GF

The Fireplace's Lava Java: V, V+, DF, GF

Wade Water: V, V+, DF, GF

FRY STATION SAFETY TIPS

If you're making something that requires deep frying, here are some important tips to prevent any kitchen fires:

- If you don't have a dedicated deep fryer, use a Dutch oven or a high-walled sauté pan.
- Never have too much oil in the pan! You don't want hot oil spilling out as soon as you put the food in.
- Only use a suitable cooking oil, like canola, peanut, or vegetable oil.
- Always keep track of the oil temperature with a thermometer—350°F to 375°F should do the trick.
- Never put too much food in the pan at the same time!
- Never put wet food in the pan. It will splatter and may cause burns.
- Always have a lid nearby to cover the pan in case it starts to spill over or catch fire. A properly rated fire extinguisher is also great to have on hand in case of emergencies.
- Never leave the pan unattended, and never let children near the pan.
- Never, ever put your face, hand, or any other body part in the hot oil.

CONVERSION CHART

Kitchen Measurements

CUPS	TABLESPOONS	TEASPOONS	FLUID OUNCES
¹⁄₁₆ cup	1 Tbsp	3 tsp	½ fl oz
⅛ cup	2 Tbsp	6 tsp	1 fl oz
¼ cup	4 Tbsp	12 tsp	2 fl oz
⅓ cup	5½ Tbsp	16 tsp	2⅔ fl oz
½ cup	8 Tbsp	24 tsp	4 fl oz
⅔ cup	10⅔ Tbsp	32 tsp	5⅓ fl oz
¾ cup	12 Tbsp	36 tsp	6 fl oz
1 cup	16 Tbsp	48 tsp	8 fl oz

GALLONS	QUARTS	PINTS	CUPS	FLUID OUNCES
¹⁄₁₆ gal	¼ qt	½ pt	1 cup	8 fl oz
⅛ gal	½ qt	1 pt	2 cups	16 fl oz
¼ gal	1 qt	2 pt	4 cups	32 fl oz
½ gal	2 qt	4 pt	8 cups	64 fl oz
1 gal	4 qt	8 pt	16 cups	128 fl oz

Weight

GRAMS	OUNCES
14 g	½ oz
28 g	1 oz
57 g	2 oz
85 g	3 oz
113 g	4 oz
142 g	5 oz
170 g	6 oz
283 g	10 oz
397 g	14 oz
454 g	16 oz
907 g	32 oz

Oven Temperatures

FAHRENHEIT	CELSIUS
200°F	93°C
225°F	107°C
250°F	121°C
275°F	135°C
300°F	149°C
325°F	163°C
350°F	177°C
375°F	191°C
400°F	204°C
425°F	218°C
450°F	232°C

Length

IMPERIAL	METRIC
1 in	2.5 cm
2 in	5 cm
4 in	10 cm
6 in	15 cm
8 in	20 cm
10 in	25 cm
12 in	30 cm

GLOSSARY

Beat: To blend ingredients and/or incorporate air into a mixture by vigorously whisking, stirring, or using a handheld or stand mixer.

Blender: Blends or purées sauces and soups to varying textures, from chunky to perfectly smooth. Also used to make smoothies and shakes.

Butter: Unless otherwise noted, recipes call for salted butter.

Butterfly Pea Flowers: These dried flower blossoms are commonly used in herbal tea drinks. When added to a recipe, they provide a beautiful deep blue color. If combined with acids, like lemon juice, the color turns to pink or purple. They are available online and in some health food stores. They are also turned into a powder and an extract.

Candy Thermometer: Sometimes called fry thermometers, these long glass thermometers can be clipped to the side of a pot. They can withstand temperatures of at least 500°F and are used to measure the temperatures of frying oil or sugar when making syrups, candies, and certain frostings.

Colander: Separates liquids from solids by draining the liquid through the small holes in the bowl.

Cutting In Butter: To work cold butter into dry ingredients until it is broken down into small pea-sized pieces and dispersed evenly throughout the mixture. It is important that the butter is very cold so it does not begin to soften. These little pieces of butter surrounded by the dry ingredients are what create the flakiness in pastry.

Dry Measuring Cups: Measuring tools that usually come in sets of ¼ cup, ⅓ cup, ½ cup, and 1 cup sizes. They are ideal for measuring dry ingredients such as flour, sugar, rice, and pasta.

Dutch Oven: A large (usually 5- to 6-quart) heavy cooking pot ideal for making stews, braises, and deep-fried foods. Dutch ovens are often made from cast iron or enameled cast iron, which makes them hold and distribute heat evenly. A Dutch oven works well when cooking with both high and low temperatures, making it a versatile vessel and handy addition to every kitchen.

Egg Wash: A mixture used to create a sheen or gloss on breads, pastries, and other baked goods. Whisk together 1 egg and 1 tablespoon of water until light and foamy. Use a pastry brush to apply before baking when the recipe requires.

Folding In: This refers to gently adding an ingredient with a spatula in wide, gentle strokes. Do not whisk or stir vigorously. Folding allows any airiness already established to stay intact.

Food Processor: A motorized machine with a bowl and a series of removable blades used for chopping, shredding, slicing, and blending ingredients. A food processor can be used to prepare vegetables, fruits, and cheeses for cooking as well as for blending sauces and dips.

Frying Pan: Shallow round cooking vessel used primarily for stovetop cooking. It's good to have a range of sizes. Generally, a small frying pan or skillet is 6 inches across; a medium skillet is 8 inches across; a large skillet is 10 inches across; and an extra-large skillet is 12 inches across.

Granulated Sugar: A highly refined sugar made from sugar cane or beets known for its white color and fine texture. All of the molasses has been removed from this type of sugar.

Greasing a Pan: Coating a pan with nonstick cooking spray, oil, softened butter, or shortening to keep (usually) baked goods such as cakes from sticking.

Hand Mixer: A lightweight handheld machine with removable attachments used for blending and whipping eggs, cake batters, and lighter-weight, less dense doughs.

High-Heat vs. Nonstick Pans: A high-heat pan—as its name suggests—can stand up to high-heat cooking, generally temperatures between 400°F and 600°F. They're usually made of stainless steel, cast iron, or enameled cast iron and can be used on the stovetop or in the oven—if the handle is made of an ovenproof material.

Nonstick cookware contains a coating that helps keep foods from sticking (particularly eggs), but they can't be used at the same temperatures as high-heat pans. If you are cooking with nonstick cookware, make sure you know the manufacturer's heat limits for your cookware. Most nonstick cookware should not be used at above medium heat on a stovetop (about 350°F) and is not generally suitable for the oven.

Immersion Blender: A handheld machine used for puréeing soups and sauces in the pot.

Liquid Measuring Cup: Clear glass or plastic measuring tools used for measuring precise amounts of liquids by lining up the level of liquid to the marks on the cup. Useful sizes include 1 cup, 2 cup, and 4 cup.

Measuring Spoons: A set of measuring tools used to accurately portion smaller amounts of ingredients. They usually come in a set that includes ⅛ teaspoon, ¼ teaspoon, ½ teaspoon, 1 teaspoon, and 1 tablespoon. They can be used for liquid ingredients such as vinegar, juices, oils, and extracts, and dry ingredients such as flour, salt, sugar, and spices.

Milk: Unless otherwise noted, these recipes call for dairy milk. In most cases, any percentage of milk fat will do, unless otherwise noted.

Muddler: A short-handled tool that is textured on one end used to mash together ingredients such as fruits, herbs, and sugar when making flavored drinks.

Parchment Paper: Food-safe paper that can withstand temperatures of up to 450°F—even up to 500°F for shorter baking times—that's used to line pans for baking and roasting. Parchment paper keeps foods from sticking and makes cleanup easier.

Peeling Ginger: To peel fresh gingerroot, use the edge of a small spoon to scrape away the peel. This keeps the root intact, with less waste, and allows you to easily navigate the lumps and bumps.

Piping Frosting: The process of decorating cakes and cookies by squeezing frosting placed in a decorating bag over them. Piping can be done with or without a decorating tip—or even in a plastic bag with one corner snipped off to allow the frosting to be applied in a neat rope shape.

Powdered Sugar: Also called confectioners' sugar, this is granulated sugar that has been ground into a powdered state. It's primarily used to make smooth icings and for dusting finished baked goods.

Rolling Pin: A long, cylindrical tool—most often made of wood—used to flatten and roll out dough when making breads and pastries.

Rubber Spatula: A handled tool with a flat, flexible blade used to fold ingredients together and to scrape the sides of bowls clean.

Salt: Unless otherwise noted, use your salt of choice in the recipes in this book. Kosher salt—which is coarser than regular table salt—is the type of salt that is most commonly used throughout the book.

Saucepan with Lid: Round, deep cooking vessel used for boiling or simmering. It is useful to have a range of sizes, including a 1 quart, 2 quart, 3 quart, and 4 quart.

Sear: To create a crust on a piece of meat, poultry, or fish by placing it in a very hot pan or on a very hot grill. The high heat quickly caramelizes the natural sugars in the food, creating a deeply browned and flavorful crust. Once the crust is formed, the heat is usually turned down so that the interior of the meat can cook properly before the outside is burned.

Sift: The process of putting flour, powdered sugar, or cornstarch through a fine-mesh sieve to aerate and remove lumps. Multiple ingredients—such as flour, salt, and leveningss—are often sifted together to blend them.

Silicone Baking Mat: Used to line shallow baking pans when making foods such as cookies and pastries to prevent sticking. They can withstand high temperatures in the oven and can also be used in the freezer. Dough can be rolled out on them, and they can easily go from prep station to chilling to the oven without having to move the dough. They are easy to clean and reusable.

Simmer: To cook a liquid such as a sauce or soup at low-enough heat so that bubbles are just barely breaking over the surface.

Spatula/Pancake Turner: A handled tool with a wide, flexible blade used to flip or turn foods during cooking.

Stand Mixer: A heavy-duty machine with a large bowl and various attachments used to mix, beat, or whip foods at varying speeds. Stand mixers are necessary for making heavy, dense, or stiff doughs for cookies or yeasted breads.

Vanilla Paste vs. Vanilla Extract: Vanilla bean paste provides strong vanilla flavor and beautiful vanilla bean flecks without having to split and scrape a vanilla bean. Although it is more expensive than extract, there are situations in which it really elevates the finished dish. When that's the case, a recipe will specifically call for vanilla bean paste, but it can always be replaced in a 1-to-1 ratio with vanilla extract.

Whip: To use a whisk or electric mixer to aerate ingredients such as egg whites and heavy cream to lighten, stiffen, and form peaks.

Whisk: A handled tool with thin wires arranged in various shapes used for mixing and whipping liquids and batters to combine ingredients or incorporate air into them. The two most common types of whisks are the balloon whisk, which has a bulbous end that narrows down toward the handle, and the sauce whisk, which has a round coil that sits flat on the bottom of the pan.

ABOUT THE AUTHORS

Tara Theoharis is an author and recipe developer known for her pop culture–inspired cookbooks. Titles include *Break an Egg: The Broadway Cookbook*, *Tomb Raider: The Official Cookbook and Travel Guide*, and *Minecraft: Gather, Cook, Eat! An Official Cookbook*. When not cooking, she can be found playing games and binging TV shows with her husband and two sons. www.taratheoharis.com

To my "Little Chef," Leonidas.

Special thanks to my primary taste tester and lifelong adventure buddy, Alexander Theoharis, and thank you to our fantastic editor, Anna Wostenberg, and brilliant writer, S. T. Bende, for making this book absolutely fabulous.

And thank you, Pixar, for bringing creativity and joy to us all, and making me cry within the first 20 minutes of every feature, guaranteed.

S. T. Bende is a young-adult and children's author, known for the Norse mythology series Viking Academy and The Ære Saga. She's also written books for Disney and Lucasfilm. She lives on the West Coast, where she spends far too much time at Disneyland, and she dreams of skiing on Jotunheim and Hoth. www.stbende.com.

To my favorite little racers, our family pit crew, and our treasured collection of Cars. *Do not eat the pistachio ice cream. It has turned!*

Thanks to the brilliant Tara Theoharis for bringing these films into our kitchen and to our epic editor, Anna Wostenberg, for continually letting me dive into the worlds that shape my heart. Much gratitude to the extraordinary team at Pixar for decades of inspiration . . . and for teaming up with the Disney Imagineers to give us our very own, real-life Radiator Springs. *Ka-chow!*

INDEX

NOTES

INSIGHT
EDITIONS

PO Box 3088
San Rafael, CA 94912
www.insighteditions.com

Find us on Facebook: www.facebook.com/InsightEditions

Follow us on Instagram: @insighteditions

ISBN: 978-1-64722-970-2

Publisher: Raoul Goff
VP, Group Publisher: Vanessa Lopez
VP, Creative: Chrissy Kwasnik
VP, Manufacturing: Alix Nicholaeff
VP, Senior Executive Project Editor: Vicki Jaeger
Publishing Director: Jamie Thompson
Designer: Brooke McCullum
Senior Editor: Anna Wostenberg
Editorial Assistant: Sami Alvarado
Managing Editor: Maria Spano
Senior Production Editor: Nora Milman
Production Associate: Deena Hashem
Senior Production Manager, Subsidiary Rights: Lina s Palma-Temena

Photography by Ted Thomas
Props and food styling by Elena P. Craig

ROOTS of PEACE   REPLANTED PAPER

Insight Editions, in association with Roots of Peace, will plant two trees for each tree used in the manufacturing of this book. Roots of Peace is an internationally renowned humanitarian organization dedicated to eradicating land mines worldwide and converting war-torn lands into productive farms and wildlife habitats. Roots of Peace will plant two million fruit and nut trees in Afghanistan and provide farmers there with the skills and support necessary for sustainable land use.

Manufactured in China by Insight Editions

10 9 8 7 6 5 4 3 2 1